GOD'S KINGDOM

GOD'S KINGDOM
A Guide for Biblical Study

GEORGE V. PIXLEY

Translated from the Spanish
by Donald D. Walsh

ORBIS BOOKS
Maryknoll, New York 10545

First published as *Reino de Dios,* copyright © 1977 Asociación Editorial La Aurora, Doblas 1753-1424, Buenos Aires, Argentina

English translation, including revisions, copyright © 1981 by Orbis Books, Maryknoll, NY 10545

Manufactured in the United States of America

Library of Congress Cataloging in Publication Data

Pixley, George V.
  God's kingdom.

  Translation of: Reinos de Dios.
  Includes bibliographical references and index.
  1. Kingdom of God—Biblical teaching. I. Title.
BT94.P5213   231.7'2   81-3946
ISBN 0-88344-156-X (pbk.)   AACR2

CONTENTS

Foreword, by Harvey Cox   vii
Introduction   1
1. The Cultic Celebration of Yahweh's Kingship   10
2. Yahweh's Kingdom, the Political Project of the
    Israelite Tribes   19
3. Yahweh's Kingdom as the Ideology of an Israelite
    State   37
4. God's Kingdom as Hierocratic Society   55
5. God's Kingdom in First-Century Palestine   64
6. The Internationalization of God's Kingdom   88
7. What Is to Be Done?   101
Notes   106
Scripture Index   114

Foreword

"My kingdom is not of this world," said Jesus to Pilate at his trial. And what a twisted trail of confused misinterpretations and questionable applications have followed in the path of this single text. If Jesus did not intend his kingdom to come in this world, then why did he so boldly confront the rulers of this world in Jerusalem when he might have remained safely secluded in Galilee? Why did he invade the temple, the political and economic power center of his time and place, causing such a stir that the remaining events of Holy Week—his arrest, trial, condemnation, and execution—became inevitable? Why does the last book of the New Testament confidently foretell that it is the kingdoms of *this* world that "shall become the kingdoms of our God and his Christ"? Above all, why does Jesus instruct his disciples to pray for the coming of God's Kingdom "on earth as it is in heaven"?

Throughout Christian history the argument over just how earthly the Kingdom of God is supposed to be has been fought along quite predictable lines. Those who are rich or content or powerful or comfortable here and now prefer a kingdom to come that will not alter our earthly reality very soon or very much. They like it the way it is now. They have devised theologies of inward, figurative, or post-historical kingdoms, or kingdoms that begin only after death. No

vii

wonder. The powerful would prefer their "casting down" that Mary sings of in the Magnificat to happen in some other world, not this one. The rich, reading of the woes that Jesus promises them in Luke's Gospel, have an equally understandable preference that such woes be inward and psychological, something a skilled therapist can help them cope with. No outward or worldly woes, please.

The disinherited, on the other hand, have frequently insisted on a much more commonsensical and straightforward reading of what Jesus was saying and doing. When he speaks of emptying the prisons, they refuse to reduce this to "spiritual prisons," since the cell blocks they and their friends and loved ones languish in are made of stone and steel. When he talks about cancelling debts, they think first of all not of infractions of social decorum but of their unpaid bills and the hot breath of their creditors. When he speaks of filling the hungry, they think not of communion wafers, but of rice and beans and bread: "Thy kingdom . . . on earth."

Who has been right and who wrong in this age-old hermeneutical class struggle? Not surprisingly, since most scholars and theologians for most of history have worked for the privileged and not for the poor, the weight of scribal evidence seems to be on the side of the wealthy and well-situated. Books and articles and monographs have piled up over the centuries to document and demonstrate the transcendental or interior character of the Kingdom Jesus said was at hand. The theological ideologues of the ruling elites have poured contempt on the "crude," and "literalistic," or—still worse—the "utopian" wrong-headedness of the poor's demand that the promised milk and honey should be something hungry people can actually eat and drink.

The elite version of what the Kingdom means has held sway, with several important exceptions, for centuries of Christian theological history. But recently it has come in for a serious challenge. This book by George Pixley is at once eloquent evidence and an erudite expression of that challenge. Pixley has not only looked at the issue through the eyes of the poor (an angle of vision made possible by his life of work in Latin America) but has utilized the most refined tools of critical scholarship to lay out his case. No thoughtful reader can ever again dismiss the interpretation he advances as simplistic or unlettered. To my mind, in fact, he clinches the case: from now on those who take the traditional elite view of what the "Kingdom of God" means in the Bible will have the burden of proof.

Perhaps in describing what Pixley has done one should use the word "inquiry" rather than "case." He is interested in something far more important and more profound than simply winning an argument. To his credit he does not want merely to prove his scholarly case against someone else's, the all-too-familiar contest in academic one-upmanship. Rather, what Pixley wants to do is to ask this question: "Is the Kingdom of God preached by Jesus good news for the poor today?" His historical exploration of what Jesus and the movement around him meant by the Kingdom of God is thus not just the leisurely pursuit of an antiquarian. It is a real question, urgently asked by millions of real people today. It is not by any means a rhetorical question, and, for Pixley, the answer is far from obvious. The book leaves the reader not with the comfortable feeling that a question has been decisively answered; rather it leaves one with the troubled feeling that a far more important question has been unavoidably asked.

"Not of this world?" What did Jesus mean? That in God's Kingdom no one would "lord it over" others as he had said earlier? That God and not some worldly intermediary—Temple or Emperor—would rule in human hearts and communities? Whatever Jesus meant, Pixley believes that the question of whether the message of that reign is good news for the poor today must be answered on the plane of present historical and political engagement and not in the realm of past historical research, even research as skilled and as winsomely presented as his.

I have an advantage over the reader who is just picking up this splendid new contribution to the growing body of excellent biblical scholarship that is strengthening the liberation theology movement. Since Pixley has served as rector of the Baptist Seminary of Mexico where I have taught off and on during the past half decade, I discussed many of the ideas in this book while it was in the making. Even then I could see that Pixley, who is not only an accomplished biblical scholar but also a Christian with a burning commitment to the Latin American liberation struggle, was on to something important. Since receiving the galleys from the publisher several months back I have had a chance to share its ideas with students in my classes and seminars at Harvard. I can assure anyone who foresees using the book in such a setting that it goes over remarkably well. Inundated by scholarly books with little political relevance or with political ones that often lack scholarly depth, students find this volume a welcome surprise. It also helps students to see that even though, understandably, the leading voices in Latin American liberation theology are those of our Roman Catholic colleagues, still Protestants are beginning to play a vital role too. For all these and many more reasons it is a special joy for me to introduce this fine book—by one who is both *amigo* and *compañero*—to an English-speaking audience. My hope is that it will enable all its readers to take a bit more seriously what it is we are really asking for when we pray, "Thy Kingdom come, on earth. . . ."

HARVEY G. COX

Introduction

The author was asked to write a word study of the biblical phrase "kingdom of God," and the present study is in response to that request. The genre of the biblical word study is well established and known to pastors and laypersons in the many Bible dictionaries in wide use among our churches. Studies of certain significant biblical words such as "love" (*agape*), "peace" (*shalom*), and "spirit" (*pneuma*) have played a role in Christian belief even at the parish level. No one can doubt the value of this kind of semantic investigation for the renewal of some of the key expressions in our Christian language, which had become stale through much use and abuse.

Nevertheless, we have learned in Latin America to be suspicious of the kind of idealism that seeks "true" concepts in their purity. Often behind the beauty and desirability of the concept in the abstract lies the intention to legitimate structures that in concrete history produce misery and oppression. No better example of this fatal disease of the mind can be found than the way in which "freedom" has been used to justify misery. In the name of freedom labor unions have been broken up (because they are said to distort the "free" play of the market by introducing "artificial" levels of wages). In the name of "scientific freedom" universities have refused to serve the needs of people, preferring to devote their research facilities to the novel and complicated machinery that interests the transnational corporations. In the name of professional freedom doctors struck against the Popular Unity government in Chile seeking the right to serve whom they chose (concealing the fact that they chose to serve those who could pay best). In the name of the freedom of the marketplace price controls have been resisted always and everywhere by merchants large and small. In principle, of course, nobody can be against the freedom of human persons. However, freedom or any other concept or value never encounters us in the abstract but rather in terms of some particular historical project. And in terms of that project it may contribute to the struggle for life and salvation, or it may serve merely to justify and conceal the destruction of life.

For this reason, our study of the biblical phrase "kingdom of God" begins with the suspicion that if it were investigated in its purity as "the biblical concept of the kingdom of God" it would be easily usable for purposes not favorable to the lives of God's people. We shall confirm in our study of the Bible that there is no "biblical concept" of the kingdom of God. That God, some God, however conceived, rules the world is a very widespread idea, and certainly not limited to the Bible. Within the Bible this idea is central. However, the idea has no existence in its purity as an abstraction. It must always find expression in some particular historical project, a project that may well exclude other projects that also claim to embody the kingdom of God. We would, then, give a fundamentally false impression if we did a study of the kingdom of God in the Bible in abstraction from the particular historical embodiments that that idea found. For a Christian people that wishes to follow Jesus in a particular historical circumstance, the historical embodiments of the idea are necessary for our guidance. We do not want to follow beautiful dreams that may exist only in our heads, but to find guidance for the way to a better world where we can live more fully as sons and daughters of our God.

We shall not study the phrase "kingdom of God," then, in order to identify a supposedly pure concept. We are not interested in concepts except as they serve to guide us toward salvation—real, concrete, historical salvation. What we seek with this study of the kingdom of God in the Bible is to know both how such a fundamental notion guided the people of Israel toward a free and just society and how it was used to submit the people of Israel to tyranny under Solomon. We shall see how God's kingdom was a call by Jesus to struggle for a better life for Galilean peasants, and how it became an unhistorical ideal for the unclassed peoples of the cities of Asia Minor and Greece. In other words, we shall see how the idea of God's kingdom was used in the Bible both for good (salvation) and for ill (oppression). We do so in full awareness of the historical struggles in which Christians in Latin America are engaged, and of the need to put our faith in the service of the historical redemption of our Latin American peoples.

In undertaking the study of the phrase "kingdom of God" we are not just looking at one among many biblical ideas. This is a foundational idea: The announcement of the imminence of the arrival of God's kingdom was the main content of Jesus' preaching. Everything Jesus said and did can be subsumed under his urgent conviction that the kingdom of God was at hand. Many studies have been devoted to clarifying exactly what he meant. But in general not enough attention has been given to the fact that Yahweh's kingdom is the seminal idea of the Old Testament, so that Jesus was not preaching something new, but announcing a hope with a long history in Israel. If it is true that we cannot understand the kingdom of God in abstraction from its concrete historical embodiments, it is also true that we cannot understand the first-century hopes pinned on it without understanding its particular history in Israel.

Palestine in the century that we now call the first of the Christian Era was one of the major centers of revolt against the empire that the Romans had built on slave labor. The inspiration for this rebellion came from the holy writings of the Jews. Yahweh's kingdom, proclaimed by the prophets, was the utopia that inspired peasant masses in their resistance to Roman Domination. As one would expect in such a situation, several groups attempted to interpret the oppressed situation of the people, and each proposed its own strategy for overcoming that situation. Zealots, Essenes, Pharisees, and "Christians" all tried to channel the people's rebellion with the use of biblical categories. Only the Sadducees understood the tradition as a support for political accommodation with the authorities then in power.

Amidst these political currents appeared John, a desert prophet of Yahweh's kingdom. He was aware of the incipient movement that had gathered around the Galilean Jesus, and from jail he challenged him with the fundamental question: "Are you the one who is to come or shall we wait for another?" Jesus' answer provides a good entry to our subject:

> Go and tell John what you hear and see: the blind receive their sight and the lame walk, lepers are cleansed and the deaf hear, and the dead are raised up, and the poor have the good news preached to them [Matt. 11:4–5].

Good news for the poor! The Galilean Messiah interpreted his powerful works on the bodies of Palestinian poor men and women as the beginning of God's kingdom, which the prophets announced as salvation for the poor and vengeance on their oppressors (Ps. 146; Isa. 11:9; 61:1-3). Nevertheless, the solitary prophet was executed in his imprisonment, and shortly afterward the Galilean Messiah was also executed.

Jesus' death did not finish his movement. Out of that movement came the Christian church, which is still a factor in our history. However, we do not know whether this continuation was good or bad news for the poor to whom Jesus had announced a coming kingdom of justice and peace. Forty years later Mark wrote a "gospel" in the midst of the chaos of the Judeo-Roman War (A.D. 66-70).[1] Recalling words of Jesus, he announced the near solution to all the people's aspirations: "Truly, I say to you, there are some standing here who will not taste death before they see the kingdom of God come with power" (Mark 9:1).

Yet in less than three hundred years the church born in a Palestine on fire with rebellion was embracing the Roman Empire under the leadership of the "Christian Emperor" Constantine. History would provide new expressions of this marriage between the hope of God's kingdom and the class societies of this world. When the Spanish Empire reached America in the sixteenth century, it was accompanied by a supporting Christian church. In the nineteenth and twentieth centuries, when United States imperialism penetrated into Latin America, it was accompanied by Protestant missions.

This tragic history cannot be brushed aside. It must be understood. Was it a betrayal of a potentially liberating rebel movement, or was the movement of Jesus the Messiah from its beginning a false announcement of freedom for the oppressed? Today in Latin America we are witnessing the birth of a rebel church that identifies with the struggles of oppressed people against their exploiters. It is essential for this struggle that we examine anew the sources of Christian faith. The Bible has often been used against the lives of ordinary working people. If this is not to happen again we must know our sources and their potential for good and for ill.

According to the Gospels, the people of Jerusalem initially received Jesus as the Messiah they had been awaiting. Surrounded by a multitude of jubilant well-wishers, Jesus and his following of Galileans entered the Temple to face the priestly hierarchy that was "doing business" there. In the short span of a week's time, the people of Jerusalem changed positions. When given a choice, they preferred the Zealot Barabbas to the Messiah Jesus of Nazareth.

We must seriously ask ourselves whether this crowd understood correctly its interests. Later history showed the limitations of the Zealot option. The multitudes followed the leadership of the Zealots into the war of 66–70 and saw Titus lead his legions into the city of Jerusalem and destroy its Temple. The Zealots, then, were not the answer. But would the crowd have done any better by choosing to follow Jesus? Would they have achieved freedom from Roman domination? Could the tragedy have been avoided that the Christian church has meant for the working peoples of the world? This matter is not of purely academic interest. The rebellious church that emerges from the Latin American people tries to join forces with the working people of the cities and the countryside against their oppressors—and also against a church that is allied to the oppressors. This strategy is valid only if it is possible to recover in the Bible a political and religious current that will give the lie to the church of the powerful and genuinely offer good news for ordinary working people. This is what is at stake in a study of the biblical history of the idea of God's kingdom.

But study alone will not be sufficient to answer so momentous a historical question. It is the hope of the author of this small book that it will motivate Christian groups to study the Scriptures that inspired those defeated rebellions against the Roman Empire in search of guidance for the different struggles of our time. This is a new kind of Bible study. It is not an exercise of Christian devotion. Nor is it an objective, scientific, intellectual exercise. The Bible study we need must question our faith in the light of the strategic requirements of the struggle for life and freedom. The theme of God's kingdom is exciting because of its importance in the beginnings of the church and because many believe it is relevant to the struggle that we are today carrying on for a just social order. But we do not know that it is genuinely relevant. The author as a professional of biblical studies does not know. Collectively, we Latin American Christians do not know. Only the working people in their struggle for life will prove or disprove that the kingdom of God is good news for the poor. It is this vital concern that moves Christian people to investigate again God's kingdom in the Bible.

This study is divided for convenience into six parts. Each unit could be called an adventure of God's kingdom. That is, we want to study this idea historically, in its various embodiments. Only thus can we determine the advisability of striving for a new embodiment in our generation. The six chapters of our study are the following:

1. The celebration of Yahweh's kingdom in the cult as revealed in the Psalms and by the prophets. This is probably the least important incorporation of Yahweh's kingdom. But it is also the most religious one, and that closest to the beliefs of neighboring peoples. God was celebrated as king in the royal cult of Jerusalem, and the texts of this cult, the Psalms, had a lasting influence on the Jewish and Christian religions.

2. Having looked at the religious meaning of Yahweh's

kingdom in monarchic times, we shall next study the role of that kingdom as the revolutionary project of the peasants of the Canaanite hills in the formation of the nation Israel. This is the first and normative incarnation of God's kingdom. All the later history of the idea must measure itself against this original historical expression.

3. The revolutionary project of Israel was after some two centuries domesticated into a class society not unlike those from which Israel had escaped in Egypt and Canaan. In this third chapter we shall document the use of God's kingdom as the official ideology of the Davidic state in the tenth to the sixth centuries before Christ.

4. When the Davidic monarchy was destroyed it was succeeded by a class society in which a priestly caste dominated the working people of the land. This hierocratic society also had a use for the idea of God's kingdom.

5. With the Zealots and with Jesus, God's kingdom again became the political project of justice and freedom for the working people of Palestine, and especially of Galilee. In the new context of a slave society, the attempt was made to again incarnate God's kingdom as a hope for the poor. After the period studied in the second chapter, this is second in importance in the biblical history of God's kingdom.

6. Finally, we shall see how God's kingdom was preached by the Christian successors of Jesus who had left the territory of Galilee where his historical vision had taken shape. Under the leadership of the missionary Paul, the kingdom became a spiritual kingdom, a shift of basic consequence for the church through the centuries.

We shall end by suggesting some tasks for today's Christian communities. This book is of necessity provisional and unfinished. It needs to be completed through the analyses and strategies of the people that still considers itself Christian even if it is not sure that this is good news. Even more, it needs to be completed by the struggle for life and justice for the working people of the world, a struggle that alone will show whether God's kingdom is a hopeful promise or a dangerous illusion.

To send forth a little book like this one, addressed to groups of churches, assumes that Christian people are capable of a critical study of their Scriptures. If this turns out not to be the case, we as Christians shall have little to offer a people that needs to criticize all its social foundations— economic, political, and cultural—since all have been converted into instruments of its oppression.

1

The Cultic Celebration
of Yahweh's Kingship

As a first approximation to our topic, let us examine how the kingship of Yahweh was celebrated in Israel as revealed in the Psalms and by the prophets. In this chapter of our study, we shall be looking at the relatively ahistorical sphere of worship, where the emphasis falls less on God's kingdom as a social, political sphere, than on his kingship abstracted from the social relations among people. This is only a relative matter, but an important one because it allowed the people of this period to appreciate Yahweh their God as king in abstraction from the particularities of their national history, something Israelites could not do in the social-historical cult of earlier times. This kind of idealist abstraction, which seems so natural for religious practice, is what we have learned in Latin America to suspect as a concealment of real, historical domination. But in this chapter we wish only to make a first approximation to our subject. So we leave aside for the time being the question of the historical meaning of this praise of Yahweh as king and accept it on the same level of abstraction with which it was treated in Israel's hymns and prayers.

The celebration of God as king is a common motif of ancient Near Eastern religion. Outside of Israel, the motif was well known in Egypt, Canaan, Greece, Anatolia, and Mesopotamia. The distinctiveness of Israel in this matter is no more than a matter of emphasis. Substantively, we are dealing with a common Middle Eastern religious pattern.

In Babylon, as for many traditional peoples, there was a major annual festival whose purpose was to celebrate order and creation. This was a twelve-day festival of the New Year. One of the major motifs of this annual celebration was the renewed enthronement of Marduk as king of the gods. According to Babylonian myth, Marduk became king of the gods in virtue of his victory in combat over the forces of chaos personified in Tiamat, the monster of the seas.[2] Every New Year this victory was re-enacted both in the recitation of the myth and its ritual representation. Through the festival the Babylonian people were reassured that, whatever may have happened in the old year, order was now restored by Marduk's secure possession of kingship.

It is likely that in pre-exilic Israel a similar annual festival of creation and divine kingship was also celebrated. The biblical texts do not offer systematic information on Israelite festivals until the priestly codifications of the post-exilic epoch, but much can be pieced together from the occasional references in the historical works, and most especially from the hymns collected in the book of Psalms. From the latter we learn that the myth of God's kingship and creation by means of his primal victory over the forces of chaos was known in Israel in a form that resembled the Enuma Elish. Note how the motifs of creation, victory over the chaos/the sea monster, and Yahweh's kingship are combined in Psalm 74:12–17:[3]

Yet God my King is from of old,
working salvation in the midst of the earth.

Thou didst divide the sea by thy might;
thou didst break the heads of the dragons on the
    waters.
Thou didst crush the heads of Leviathan,
thou didst give him as food for the creatures of the
    wilderness.
Thou didst cleave open springs and brooks;
thou didst dry up ever-flowing streams.
Thine is the day, thine also the night;
thou hast established the luminaries and the sun.
Thou hast fixed all the bounds of the earth;
thou hast made summer and winter.

From this and other biblical references to God's primal victory over chaos it is evident that there was an Israelite form
of the Babylonian creation myth. The Genesis versions of
creation were not the only ones in Israel.

Of course this does not yet prove the existence of an annual festival like the Babylonian one. The liturgical calen-
dars of the post-exilic priestly writers (Lev. 23 and Num.
28–30) do indeed mention a festival of trumpets on the first
day of the seventh month, a festival which in the rabbinical
writings was taken to be a New Year's festival. The rabbinical writings, put together after the destruction of the Temple in A.D. 70, tell us that the kingship of God was the theme
of this festival.[4] This is almost certainly due to the preservation of the major theme of the ancient Israelite New Year.

The direct evidence for the nature of the ancient Israelite
festival of creation/New Year is to be found in the Psalms.
We take the Psalms to be for the most part liturgical pieces
from the period of the Jerusalem monarchy.[5] As such they
bear witness to the temple liturgy, not so much by describing
the action as by providing the words with which the celebra-

tion was expressed. The Psalms contain various references to a procession of Yahweh the king:

> Lift up your heads, O gates!
> and be lifted up, O ancient doors!
> that the King of glory may come in.
> Who is this King of glory?
> Yahweh Sebaot, he is the King of glory![6]
> [Psalm 24:9–10].

In the procession that is presupposed in this text, Yahweh the king approaches the gates (of the Temple?) and a dialogue ensues with the guardians of the entrance, the purpose of which is to identify the "king of glory." From another psalm we can learn that the presence of Yahweh the king was represented by the "ark of the covenant," an ancient sacred object from premonarchic times which represented the throne of the divine king:

> Let us go to his dwelling place;
> let us worship at his footstool!
> Arise, Yahweh, and go to thy resting place,
> thou and the ark of thy might [Psalm 132:7–8].

Yahweh's "resting place," it is made clear in this psalm, is Mount Zion, where the Temple had been built. Here the divine king was enthroned in a solemn procession, probably on an annual basis. By this means the defeat of all the chaotic powers at the time of creation was remembered and re-enacted, and the created order reaffirmed.

There is a group of biblical psalms that specifically praise Yahweh on the occasion of his enthronement. These psalms (Pss. 47, 93, 95–99) were apparently composed for use in

the enthronement procession of Yahweh in Jerusalem,
which must have resembled Marduk's enthronement in the
Babylonian annual creation festival.[7] Yahweh demon-
strated his kingly power by taming and ruling the seas,
much as Marduk did (Pss. 29 and 93). Yahweh's kingship is
different from Marduk's in that his rule is not a lordship
over the gods but over the nations of the earth:

> Clap your hands, all peoples!
> shout to God with loud songs of joy!
> For Yahweh, the Most High, is terrible,
> a great king over all the earth.
> He subdued peoples under us,
> and nations under our feet.
> He chose our heritage for us,
> the pride of Jacob whom he loves.
> God has gone up with a shout,
> Yahweh with the sound of a trumpet. . . .
> For Yahweh is king of all the earth;
> sing praises with a psalm!
> Yahweh reigns over the nations;
> God has taken his seat on his holy throne.[8]
> The princes of the peoples gather
> as the people of the God of Abraham.
> For the shields of the earth belong to Yahweh,
> he is highly exalted! [Psalm 47].

In the hymnic phrases of this psalm we can clearly discern
the procession by means of which Yahweh (and his ark) are
led to the throne room, where he takes his place as king of
the nations. The cultic procession of Yahweh resembles the
processions of Canaanite and Babylonian gods. For these
other nations, however, the created order was secured by
the king-god's rule over heaven. Yahweh rules over the na-

tions of earth.[9] This is rooted in Israel's history, in the experience of early Israel as being Yahweh's kingdom. We shall look more closely at that experience in the second chapter. For the moment, we note that even in the ahistorical area of the cult, Israel's historical experience left a small mark.

The immediate context for the "religious" understanding of Yahweh's kingship is the sphere of Canaanite religion. Canaanite religion is now well known to us from the Ugaritic library of the fourteenth century B.C., which was discovered at Ras Shamra. In the mythological texts from Ugarit the royal title is reserved for the god El, the father of the gods. Nevertheless, Baal also exerts authority over the gods and he also has a palace. El and Baal correspond to two types of celestial gods well known in the mythologies of several of the peoples of the world.[10] El corresponds to the highest god, identified with the cloudless sky. According to Eliade's typology, this royal figure rules by means of his word. He sits on his throne and allows his powerful spells to control the other gods. The other celestial god is represented by the stormy sky. He is a warrior, a virile king who reigns because he has defeated his enemies with his might. In Indian mythology the two celestial types are present in the gods Varuna and Indra.

The Yahweh who defeated Leviathan, the sea monster, and ascended to his throne in solemn procession so that order was restored to the nations, appears to belong to the second type of celestial god. But there are many biblical texts that present Yahweh instead as serene in his sovereignty, seated securely on his throne, emitting decrees, much in the manner of El. So he appeared to Isaiah in his inaugural vision (Isa. 6) and to the prophet Micaiah in his vision of the heavenly court (1 Kings 22). This is the God who judged the gods in Psalm 82, and the one who rules his court in Job 1. It is also the creator god of the priestly crea-

tion story in Gen. 1. Yahweh, then, is a complex kingly figure who combines features of the Canaanite gods El and
Baal. The specifics of Yahweh's kingship can be clarified
only later when we examine Israel's historical experience of
Yahweh's kingdom.

One of the elements of the common Near Eastern celebration of the high god's kingship that received special emphasis in Israel's worship was the responsibility of the
heavenly king for establishing and maintaining justice. The
biblical psalms celebrate Yahweh's enthronement because it
will mean the overthrow of the forces of injustice personified by the sea monster.[11] The emotional tone of the annual
festival is that of joy, and in the accompanying psalms the
nations of earth clap their hands at Yahweh's enthronement
because it will mean the establishment of justice and the
liberation of the oppressed:

> Yahweh reigns; let the earth rejoice;
> let the many coastlands be glad!
> Clouds and thick darkness are round about him;
> righteousness and justice are the foundation of his
>   throne.
> Fire goes before him,
> and burns up his adversaries round about.
> His lightnings lighten the world;
> the earth sees and trembles.
> The mountains melt like wax before Yahweh,
> before the lord of all the earth.
> The heavens proclaim his righteousness;
> and all the peoples behold his glory.
> Yahweh loves those who hate evil;
> he preserves the lives of his faithful ones;
> he delivers them from the hand of the wicked
>
> > [Psalm 97:1–6, 10].

Let the sea roar, and all that fills it;
the world and those who dwell in it!
Let the floods clap their hands;
let the hills sing for joy together before Yahweh
for he comes to judge the earth.
He will judge the world with righteousness,
and the peoples with equity [Psalm 98:7-9].

Judgment is part of a king's task, and judgment here means
to subdue the wicked and to free from their dominion those
who trust in Yahweh.

This motif of Yahweh as the king who comes to right the
wrongs of the world is related to another more strictly
Israelite legal emphasis on the rights of the orphan, the widow, and the resident foreigner. Yahweh in his epiphany as
the serenely enthroned sovereign (like the Canaanite El) is
held responsible for the protection of the weak within his
kingdom. According to the surprising Psalm 82 it is precisely this which makes him God, and it is because the other
so-called gods do not right the wrongs of this world that
they expose themselves as not gods. There are parallels to
this Israelite legal preference for the widows, the orphans,
and the resident foreigners, but the particular historical experience of Israel gave special emphasis here.[12]

For the sake of completeness in our study of the celebration of Yahweh's kingship, we may briefly look at the maca-
bre cult of the divine king in a sanctuary called Tofet in the
valley of Ben Hinnom near Jerusalem.[13] There children
were sacrificed by fire in order to placate the anger of
Yahweh the King (in Hebrew, *melek*). The evidence for the
practice of such a grotesque form of worship in Israel points
only to the last decades of the Kingdom of Judah, a time of
calamitous difficulties. Both Jeremiah, who was an eye-wit-
ness to this cult, and the Holiness Code (Lev. 17-26) regard

this as a particularly shameful episode in Israel's religion.[14] From the point of view of the faithful, it was an attempt to show the depth of their obedience to the heavenly sovereign. We can imagine that they were perhaps inspired by the story of how Abraham was asked by Yahweh to sacrifice his own son Isaac (even though later a substitute was provided).[15]

The legal foundation for this cult was an ancient law: "The first-born of your sons you shall give me" (Exod. 22:28b; Eng. 22:29b). According to an old interpretation, what the law demanded was that every human first-born male be "redeemed" with a lamb (Exod. 13:11–13). This was standard Israelite practice. But in a period of great anxiety there arose the belief that Yahweh the king would be pleased with a more strict fulfillment of the law. Once the crisis had passed, the Jewish community definitively repudiated this rite directed to honor Yahweh as king, and we hear no more of it.[16]

To sum up, in the religion of Israel as in those of other Near Eastern peoples it was common to worship God as heavenly king. The biblical psalms, hymns, and prayers of temple worship in Jerusalem reveal that Yahweh was solemnly enthroned as king in a procession that shows parallels with the Babylonian Akitu festival. This cult was accompanied by a mythology that showed Yahweh creating the world and ascending his throne in mighty acts of valor against the evil power of the Sea. Bracketed in the area of the cult, Yahweh's kingship was an abstraction available for good as for ill. In order to see what this abstraction really meant for Israelite men and women we must turn to Israel's historical experience.

2

Yahweh's Kingdom, the Political Project of the Israelite Tribes

For a correct understanding of the historical significance of the kingdom of God in the Bible, the years of Israel's first formation are of the greatest importance. If we fail to grasp how Yahweh's kingdom was the concrete historical project of the tribes that organized in Canaan to withdraw together from the domination of urban states, we shall have failed to grasp the very foundation of the Christian Scriptures. Certainly, for Christians of the popular classes engaged in a struggle for life and justice this is the most hopeful and helpful moment of biblical history. Jesus' project can be rightly understood only when Israel's revolutionary project of realizing Yahweh's kingdom in the land of Canaan is first understood.

Already implied in the above paragraph is the difficulty of grasping in its historical concreteness the formation of the people of Israel. Until recently, biblical scholarship has failed to do justice to the historical significance of this experience. Modern scholars have tended to read the biblical texts looking for a history of religious ideas or, in the case of the more orthodox, a history of God's revelation (of true ideas). We have learned from our attempts at revolutionary projects that ideas accompany material reality, in the best of cases guiding and purifying it, and in the worst concealing it. We shall not be happy with biblical scholarship until it has learned to read the ideas of the Bible in terms of the historical struggles of flesh-and-blood people. This biblical scholars have begun to do. The pioneers for the study of the period of Israel's origins are Albrecht Alt in Germany some fifty years ago and George Mendenhall more recently in the United States. Since my book appeared in Spanish, Norman K. Gottwald has published what is the most important work to date on the subject.[17] Because of the unfinished state of sociological and political study on early Israel this chapter must remain somewhat tentative, but is not for that reason any less important.

Our starting point is the surprising fact that for early Israel Yahweh's kingship was taken to mean politically the exclusion of all human sovereigns. It was this rejection of human kingship that made Israel different from its neighbors. The issue is succinctly stated by the Manassite hero Gideon:

> Then the men of Israel said to Gideon, "Rule over us, you and your son and your grandson also; for you have delivered us out of the hand of Midian." Gideon said to them, "I will not rule over you, and my son will not rule over you; Yahweh rules over you" [Judg. 8:22–23].

The text is clear: If Yahweh is the king of Israel, it would be rebellion to pledge loyalty to human rulers.[18] This implication of Yahweh's kingship was never drawn for the kingship of Marduk, or that of El or Baal. These gods were generally understood to choose their favorites to reign in their cities, or to have engendered sons to serve as kings through mixed unions with human women. So it was, for instance, that Nebuchadnezzar of Babylon exercised on earth the kingship of Marduk. God's kingship in most of the ancient Near East was an ideological support for earthly states. In Israel exactly the opposite conclusion was drawn from Yahweh's kingship.

That the Gideon incident is not accidental is shown by the whole history of the relations between the free tribes of Israel and the many states that fought against Israelite autonomy. The book of Judges gathers a series of stories of popular and archaic character that tell how, time after time, the free tribes of Israel in various combinations fought against one or another Canaanite king.

At one point the southern tribes were submitted to Cushan-Rishataim, king of Edom.[19] Othniel, of the tribe of Caleb, headed a militia force that defeated Cushan-Rishataim and returned to the peasants of Israel their independence (Judg. 3:7–11).

Another time Eglon, king of Moab, oppressed some of the central tribes of Israel. This time the liberator was a certain Ehud of the tribe of Benjamin, who inspired the free Israelites to revolt by killing the Moabite King (Judg. 3:15–30).

The most important of these texts deals with the war against Jabin, "king of Canaan," and his general, Sisera, important both because of the broad alliance of Israelite tribes that it describes and because the victory over Sisera was celebrated in a hymn whose antiquity is assured by its archaic poetry (Judg. 4 and 5). According to this text several tribes of the north and the central portions of the Israelite hill country were gathered in a common military force that successfully defeated the Canaanite enemy. The leaders of this enterprise were Barak, of the tribe of Naphtali, and Deborah, of Ephraim.

Another of these ancient stories tells how Gideon, of the tribe of Manasseh, led the Israelite armed peasants against the hosts of Midian, who had domesticated camels (Judg. 6–8).

What is common to all of these military confrontations is that the men of Israel were led into battle by leaders who arose on the occasion and summoned an army to meet an occasional threat. Othniel, Ehud, Barak, and Deborah did not attempt to capitalize on their victories by building an apparatus of state power. Neither do we hear of a professional army. The kings in these confrontations are always on the other side, as are the professional military men.

The situation of Israel was evidently not easy, existing as a stateless people surrounded by Canaanite states with professional armies. So it is not surprising to hear of an early attempt to set up a human kingship in Israel, that of Abimelek of Shechem (Judg. 9). Abimelek, who was a son of Gideon of Manasseh and a woman of the city of Shechem, was proclaimed king by the people of the city and perhaps some surrounding villages (a city could not survive without the support of surrounding agricultural areas). In the context of this story of a disastrous attempt to establish kingship in Israel, a remarkable anarchist parable is told that says much about Israelite sentiment with regard to kingship (Judg. 9:7–15). According to this parable, when the trees decided to have a king they chose the olive tree for the honor. The olive tree declined, saying, "Shall I leave my fatness, by which gods and men are honored, and go to sway over the trees?" The fig and the vine responded in similar fashion when they were approached. Finally, only the bramble, who was an idle bush with nothing to contribute, could be per-

parable

suaded to take on the role of king. An eloquent testimony to
early Israel's antimonarchic sentiments!

A further commentary on the antimonarchical sentiments of the Israelites is provided by the remarkable speech
attributed to the prophet Samuel on the occasion when,
faced with constant pressure from the Philistine people on
the coastal plain, the tribes agreed to name a king. This
king, Saul of the tribe of Benjamin, was named for the sole
purpose of building a standing army to face the well-organized Philistines. He did not have a palace or the civilian
bureaucracy associated with kings in Canaan. But in the
speech of Samuel, actually composed long after the fact,
the decision to name a king is rightly seen as a fateful one:[20]

> Then all the elders of Israel gathered together and
> came to Samuel at Ramah, and said to him, "Behold,
> you are old and your sons do not walk in your ways;
> now appoint for us a king to govern us like all the na-
> tions."
>
> Samuel told all the words of Yahweh to the people
> who were asking a king from him. He said, "These are
> the ways of the king who will reign over you: he will
> take your sons and appoint them to his chariots and to
> be his horsemen, and to run before his chariots; and he
> will appoint for himself commanders of thousands
> and commanders of fifties, and some to plow his
> ground and reap his harvest, and to make his imple-
> ments of war and the equipment of his chariots. He
> will take your daughters to be perfumers and cooks
> and bakers. He will take the best of your fields and
> vineyards and olive orchards and give them to his ser-
> vants. He will take the tenth of your grain and of your
> vineyards and give it to his officers and to his servants.
> He will take your menservants and maidservants, and

the best of your cattle and your asses, and put them to his work. He will take the tenth of your flocks, and you shall be his slaves" [1 Sam. 8:4–5, 10–17].

Here we have the classic Israelite perspective on kingship: To have a king means to become slaves. The details of what this means are spelled out in terms of the monarchical states of that age. The king imposes military conscription on the young men for his army. In classical Israel there was no standing army, and the free peasants formed a fighting force only when it was necessary to face a military menace. The king also has his civilian bureaucracy, which includes the conscription of the women into the domestic service of his palace. And then there are the taxes that kings require to support the army and the civilian bureaucracy. From the perspective of free Israel, it was all unnecessary and added up to slavery.

From these texts we can take it as an established fact that not only did early Israel not have a state, but also that its existence was a deliberate rejection of states. Kingship was, in the Canaan of the thirteenth century where Israel first came into existence, a well-established social institution. In this context, for groups of peasants to declare that Yahweh their God was their only king was a conscious and dangerous political statement. It meant withdrawing from the dominant social arrangements and becoming the permanent enemy of the various states that existed in Canaan. It is this conscious political choice that has for the most part escaped biblical scholars, who, schooled in modern understandings of progress, have thought of early Israel as a primitive society that had "not yet" achieved the level of civilization required for kingship. In fact, Israelite society was a deliberate rejection of monarchy—but it was not anarchic. It had a "constitution" in its covenant (*berit*) with Yahweh.[21]

Covenants or treaties were well-established legal forms in the ancient Near East. Many have been discovered in various languages and serving various purposes. By means of covenants kings formed alliances, binding themselves by means of oaths to come to each other's assistance in case of need. Especially relevant to the covenant between Yahweh and the Israelite people is the case of what scholars have called suzerainty treaties. These are treaties imposed by a great king on a vassal king. In these legal instruments it was usual to begin by recalling the benefits that the great king had conferred on his vassal. These past benefits became grounds in the covenant for imposing future conditions on the vassal, prominent among which was exclusive loyalty to the sovereign great king. The vassal was expected to turn over fugitives from the great king, to enter into no deals with the king's enemies, and to respond to any call for military assistance. The vows that solemnized these obligations were confirmed by curses that would become effective in case of any violation. The agreement was sealed by appealing to human and divine witnesses. In general form, these are the same elements that went into Israel's covenant with Yahweh, and they can be examined in Exodus 19–24, Joshua 24, and the entire book of Deuteronomy. The heart of this covenant was the obligation upon Israel to give exclusive loyalty to Yahweh, giving service to no other god. Because of its importance, we quote at length from one of the texts that refers to the founding of Israel's legal order:

> Now therefore fear Yahweh and serve him in sincerity and in faithfulness; put away the gods which your fathers served beyond the River, and in Egypt, and serve Yahweh. And if you be unwilling to serve Yahweh, choose this day whom you will serve, whether the gods your fathers served in the region beyond the River, or the gods of the Amorites in whose land you

dwell; but as for me and my house, we will serve Yahweh.

Then the people answered, "Far be it from us that we should forsake Yahweh to serve other gods; for it is Yahweh our God who brought us and our fathers up from the land of Egypt, out of the house of bondage, and who did those great signs in our sight, and preserved us in the way that we went, and among all the peoples through whom we passed; and Yahweh drove out before us all the peoples, the Amorites who lived in the land; therefore we also will serve Yahweh, for he is our God.

But Joshua said to the people, "You cannot serve Yahweh; for he is a holy God; he is a jealous God; he will not forgive your transgressions or your sins. If you forsake Yahweh and serve foreign gods, then he will turn and harm you, and consume you, after having done you good." And the people said to Joshua, "Nay, but we will serve Yahweh."

Then Joshua said to the people, "You are witnesses against yourselves that you have chosen Yahweh to serve him." And they said, "We are witnesses." He said, "Then put away the foreign gods which are among you, and incline your heart to Yahweh the God of Israel." And the people said to Joshua, "Yahweh our God we will serve, and his voice we will obey."

So Joshua made a covenant with the people that day, and made statutes and ordinances for them at Shechem. And Joshua wrote these words in the book of the law of God; and he took a great stone, and set it up there under the oak in the sanctuary of Yahweh. And Joshua said to all the people, "Behold, this stone shall be a witness against us; for it has heard all the words of Yahweh which he spoke to us; therefore it shall be a

witness against you, lest you deal falsely with your
God."

So Joshua sent the people away, every man to his
inheritance [Josh. 24:14–28].

Every king demands exclusive loyalty from his subjects. In
this respect Yahweh is no different. The key stipulation of
this Israel's constitution is exclusive loyalty to Yahweh.

The political meaning of Israel's covenant with Yahweh
makes understandable that peculiar intolerance so characteristic of biblical religion. "You shall worship no other
god, for Yahweh, whose name is Jealous, is a jealous God"
(Exod. 34:14).[22] This, the first commandment of Israelite
law, is aimed especially against Canaanite cults. It has long
intrigued scholars of religion and has no known parallel in
the ancient Near East. Marduk was the official god of the
city of Babylon. But nothing prevented a citizen who on the
New Year celebrated Marduk as creator and king from ap-
proaching the goddess Ishtar at the hour of death or, at
some other moment, from consulting a personal or family
god. Naaman the Syrian had his gods, but on hearing that in
Israel there was a powerful prophet of Yahweh he felt no
scruples about going to consult him to seek a cure for his
leprosy (2 Kings 5). It was natural to be so tolerant, and
even David named a son for Baal (1 Chron. 14:7). Once we
see, however, the political significance of Israel's obligation
to Yahweh, the exclusiveness of their worship becomes understandable. Yahweh's demand that the people choose between him and Baal is the counterpart of the need for
peasant people in Canaan to either declare their opposition
to Canaanite kings or submit to one of them. When the
prophet Elijah forced a confrontation with the four hundred and fifty prophets of Baal on Mount Carmel, the independence of Israel was at stake (1 Kings 18:21). Confronta-

tion with Baal was also confrontation with the occupation of Israel by the Tyrians whom the queen Jezebel brought with her to Samaria. The history of prophetic confrontations with the kings of Israel and Judah must be read in the light of the first commandment and its political consequences.

But how did it come about that a sector of the population of Canaan threw off monarchy in the name of Yahweh? Where did Yahweh come from? Just who was this Yahweh anyway?

The answer to this set of questions is twofold: Canaanite class struggle and the liberation of the Hebrew slaves in Egypt. Let us postpone for the moment consideration of the division of Canaanite society into opposed classes, which made it possible for Yahweh to become the king of the peasants who rejected kingly domination. This class struggle provided the real, material base for the exclusive worship of Yahweh. However, Israelite tradition points to Moses and the group of Hebrews that he led out of slavery in Egypt as the first revelation of Yahweh. And this tradition, which is very strong in the Bible, merits serious consideration.

According to Israelite tradition, Yahweh is "your God, who brought you out of the land of Egypt, out of the house of bondage" (Exod. 20:2). The book of Exodus tells how the Hebrews were submitted to severe oppression in Egypt, engaged in the construction of storage cities. We are led to think of a condition of generalized slavery much like that with which the Temple was built in Jerusalem three centuries later. In the widespread political form of "oriental despotism" the entire population was subject to the king's call to carry out his tasks. These calls to forced labor were accepted in return for the benefits rendered by the state, when they were not excessive. But in Egypt under Ramses II they became excessive and led to the rebellion headed by Moses. As remembered by the Israelite tribes, the prelude to leaving Egypt was a repeated confrontation with the king, against whom Yahweh directed a series of severe measures, culminating in the death of the first-born of Pharaoh and his servants. As a result, Moses led the Hebrews out of Egypt and into the desert. Here he took them to the "mountain of God" to celebrate a covenant with Yahweh that would establish the conditions of life as Yahweh's kingdom.

In its present form, the exodus from Egypt has been thoroughly reworked from a pan-Israelite perspective. According to this perspective, the Hebrews were already organized in twelve tribes in Egypt, according to the twelve descendants of Jacob. Such a tribal organization, which depends on events related to the peasant uprisings in Canaan, is unthinkable in Egypt. But it is easier to say who the Egyptian Hebrews were not than who they were. Scholars have proposed that the group which Moses led out of Egypt were the tribes of Joseph, the Levites, or some other. Probably the theory that they were the group which in Canaan became the Levitical ideologists of Yahweh religion in Israel has the most to commend it, but the issue cannot be resolved at present. What does seem clear is that the Moses group contributed to Israel the faith in Yahweh the king who demanded exclusive loyalty from his people. The Israelite ideology grew out of the experience of the people Moses led out of Egypt.

By understanding the structure of the Yahwist ideology of Israel and by finding its origins, we have not finished understanding Israel as Yahweh's kingdom. In fact, the most important element, the material base that made this tribal society possible in the midst of Canaanite class societies, has not yet been explored. To this we now turn our attention.

We are relatively well informed about conditions in four-teenth-century Palestine from the correspondence discov-ered in Egypt at Tell el Amarna. This archaeological discov-ery contains the official correspondence between the Egyptian court and the many kings who governed small city-states in Canaan. Especially important for Israelite ori-gins is the constant reference in this correspondence to the presence of *'apiru*, militarized groups who threatened the stability of the Canaanite states.[23] It has long been recog-nized by scholars that *'apiru* bears a very striking re-semblance to the word for Hebrew, *'ibri*. It is most likely the same word. However, this does not mean that an Israelite nationality existed before the thirteenth century when Moses and Joshua lived. It is now the dominant opi-nion among scholars that the *'apiru* were not a nation or an ethnic group. The references to them are too diverse and are scattered over much too large an area to allow such an ex-planation. In the correspondence the word almost always refers to armed bands that are not subject to the constituted authorities, although they may serve them as mercenaries. The references are almost always pejorative. *'Apiru* ap-pears, then, to have been a sociological term rather than an ethnic one. *'Apiru* were any group that placed itself outside the law and sought its interests by means which were not acceptable to the constituted authorities.

The prominence of *'apiru* bands in the letters of Ca-naanite kings in the fourteenth century suggests that Ca-naan was living through a period of exceptional social tur-moil. Everywhere groups were leaving their places in civil society to seek betterment in other, nonlegal, channels. It is this situation of civil unrest that provided the conditions for the emergence of such a tribal, antimonarchical nation as Israel. What we have in fourteenth-century Canaan is a class struggle that had not yet taken on clear definition, but that shortly would do so under the banner of Yahweh, the God who freed the *'ivrim* from Egyptian domination through the leadership of Moses his prophet.

Besides the widespread unrest attributed by the kings to the *'apiru*, another significant conclusion to be drawn from the Tell el Amarna correspondence is the rather striking distribution of the population in the cities.[24] Dozens of cities are mentioned in the lowlands. These are the relatively fertile and flat lands that encompass the coastal plains and the valley that cuts across Canaan from just north of Mount Carmel to just south of the sea of Galilee (Valley of Megiddo, Jezreel, or Esdraelon). Each city had its king. Each had its surrounding villages. The overall effect one receives is that of a fairly dense population, highly organized in small political units. On the other hand, very little mention is made of the hill country that was to play so prominent a role in the history of Israel. Three cities are mentioned in the hills, and they seem to have dominated large but sparsely populated areas. From south to north they are Jerusalem, Shechem, and Hazor. It was this relative emptiness of the hill country where Israel was to have its center that led Alt to propose that Israel originated in bands of herdsmen who moved from the desert into the unpopulated hill slopes and then came into conflict with the settlers of the valleys as they multiplied and became stronger. However, this is not the only conclusion that can be drawn from the fact itself. It fails to account for the intensity of the struggle between Israel and Canaan or for the adoption by Israel of the exodus as its ideology and Yahweh as its god.

Recent research, summarized by Gottwald in *The Tribes of Yahweh*, pp. 435–463, has shown that pastoral nomadism was not an independent form of social organization in the ancient Near East. Rather, the care of animals was a secondary function of groups devoted primarily to agriculture. The herdsmen were integrated into the larger communities and dependent on them. The idea of groups of nomads existing on their own as autonomous social units is false to the circumstances of the time as these did not arise until the domestication of the camel.

The relatively unpopulated hills provided for the emergence of Israel in a different manner from that supposed by Alt. The hills were an area into which rebellious peasants could retreat to get away from their urban oppressors. Here we have the true class character of the struggle of Israelite free peasants with Canaanite states.

If Israel was a deliberate attempt to carry a class struggle through to the establishment of Yahweh's kingdom in the midst of Canaanite class society, we shall need some class analysis to clarify the project. The relevant category is that of the Asiatic mode of production.[25] Any society must organize in order to provide the basic necessities to reproduce itself. From the very beginning humans divide the labor necessary to produce food, clothing, and the other necessities that sustain life. The manner in which this division takes place leads to structures of society that insure the circulation of the goods produced by the different sectors of society. The accumulation of the products of human labor is only possible under conditions where this division of labor becomes a class division, in which a sector of society is able to accumulate the benefits of the labors of others. Modes of production are the various types of social organizations, both class and classless organizations that are possible and that have occurred in history.

The Asiatic, or tributary, mode of production was characteristic, in several variants, of all the civilizations of the ancient Near East. The producers of the basic material necessities in this type of society are peasants organized in villages. Village organization follows traditional patterns with leadership provided by kinship ties, the elders of families usually being the dominant figures. Possession of the land within the village is collective, with its use determined by the traditional kinship structures. The unit of production is the village, rather than the individual or the family.

Superimposed on these village units of production is the state. It draws tribute from the villages (not from taxes on individuals), in exchange for which it provides services that are sometimes economic (irrigation canals, for instance), almost always political (defense against banditry and foreign invasion), and often religious (maintenance of the symbolic center). In this mode of production there was no private ownership of the means of production. Often the king was the titular owner of all lands, so that tribute took the form of land rent. This mode of production proved to be a very stable one, which survived for millennia in places like Egypt and Mesopotamia.

The reason for its stability was the stability of its base, the village. The village had existed as a productive unit before the emergence of the state. The primitive community was not destroyed by the superimposition of the state. The ruling class was for practical purposes coterminous with the state. Different states might come and go, but the village would continue. Dynasties and empires could pass away without greatly affecting the village base of production. History was usually made by the states, who had the resources to put up monuments and send forth armies. Tribute could be exacted from the villages not just in grains but also in labor for the construction of instruments of production such as dikes against floods and also for the construction of monuments for the gods or kings.

This was the specific character of the class society from which the 'apiru seceded. Taking advantage of the competition among many relatively small states in Canaan, groups in various parts of the land withdrew to set up a classless society. This was made possible by the presence of hill country that was relatively unpopulated. The soil was not as good as that of the lowlands, but there were few kings there and the chariots that were the most frightful weapons of the time could not function well in hilly terrain. It is probable that the mastery of the technique for producing iron tools about this time also facilitated the opening of less fertile soil so that it could support human life. Finally, the arrival of the Moses group with their covenant with Yahweh who had freed them from the Egyptian king and his forced labors provided the various seceding peasant groups with a common historical project, that of building Yahweh's kingdom in Canaan.

We are now in a position to understand the covenant ceremony at Shechem, which we quoted earlier from Joshua 24. This form or one like it must have been used on different occasions to bring into Israel new groups. The presence of the Israelite tribal federation as a continuing reality in the hills must have proved an inspiration to many peasant groups who paid tribute in grain and in service to the many Canaanite kings of the plains. The very nearness of Israel would have posed a threat to these Canaanite states, which must have ardently wished to destroy this popular revolution. For it was proving that it was not indispensable to be submitted to the protection of a king. And over the years new groups joined Israel, making it necessary to have a regular way of incorporating them and providing them with the basic traditions of Israel, which would sustain them through temptations to return to one state or another for protection. This is the role of the ceremony of covenant ratification that we are given in Joshua 24.[26]

As Yahweh's kingdom, Israel had certain legal traditions that served to organize life and provide a framework for

settling disputes. Many of the laws of the Israelite tribes
were simply Israelite versions of the laws of other Near
Eastern nations. Matters like theft, murder, adultery, and
rape were dealt with in the usual ways. But some of the laws
were designed to protect the classless society that was peculiar to Israel in that territory. Special attention was paid to
those sectors of society that were exposed to becoming poor
or being abused by their neighbors:

> You shall not wrong a stranger or oppress him, for you
> were strangers in the land of Egypt. You shall not af-
> flict any widow or orphan. If you do afflict them, and
> they cry out to me [Yahweh], I will surely hear their
> cry; and my wrath will burn, and I will kill you with the
> sword, and your wives shall become widows and your
> children fatherless [Exod. 22:20–23; Eng. 22:21–24].

The laws of land tenure were derived from both village
traditions and from the Asiatic type of society, with the difference that in Israel Yahweh was king. All the land be-
longed to Yahweh. In practice this meant that the land that
was cultivated could not be bought or sold. As in traditional
village practices the land was for those who could cultivate
it. In Israelite law this peasant possession was protected by
the Jubilee: if a family had to give it up for any reason, it
was their right to get it back at the end of a fifty-year cycle
(Lev. 25). We do not know how these prescriptions were put
into practice, but their intention to make real a society
without poverty is clear.

Surely Israel's historical project represents one of the
great moments in human history. Here the people made
their own history without a leading class that was also a
class of dominators. In Yahweh's kingdom all were equals
(barring the male domination that Israel did not systemati-

cally deal with). Because this historical project was done in the presence of and over against well-organized class societies, Israel can properly be called a revolutionary society.

Still, the Israelite historical project is not unambiguous. At least it does not appear as an unambiguous good in the terms of contemporary revolutionary theory. For Israel paid for its control over its own destiny with the loss of material "progress." The free peasants who organized into independent tribes represented a step backward in material civilization with respect to Canaanite class society. It is one of the tragedies of history that class society was everywhere necessary for the accumulation of wealth that made possible great art and engineering. Israel in its period of revolutionary zeal chose human equality and freedom above civilization and material progress. Marxist revolutionary theory proposes a classless society that goes beyond capitalism, not just in humanity and justice, but also in productive capacity. It must be said that so far this is a claim that has not been substantiated in reality, but that has not been decisively disproved either. That is not the point right now. Rather it is important for us as we explore the biblical notion of the kingdom of God to realize that in its original historical expression in the Bible it put equality and justice above what we value as technology and civilization. How we value this decision is not something to be decreed by fiat. That we recognize it and the dilemma it poses does seem important.

3

Yahweh's Kingdom as the Ideology of an Israelite State

Yahweh's kingdom, made up by an expanding group of Israelite tribes settled in the hills of Canaan, lived on for more than two centuries in the face of constant hostility from the wealthier class societies that inhabited the lower lands. Some cities existed also in the hills, among the free tribes of Yahweh, but politically in sympathy with the coastal class societies. Jerusalem was one of these cities; it remained enemy territory in the Israelite heartland. The city of Shechem in the hills of Ephraim had some relations with Israel, but remained potentially an enemy and occasionally caused trouble for Israel. The city of Gibeon seems to have become, on the contrary, an ally of the Israelite experiment in a classless society (Josh. 9-10). For our purposes, the important thing to remember is that throughout the two centuries and a fraction of Israel's living out Yahweh's kingdom, the tribes never had peace with their neighbors.

And so it had to be. The Israelite tribes were the result of various movements of withdrawal of the labor force of the different Canaanite states. For their continued survival these states had to pressure Israel, if only not to lose the remaining peasant population on which they depended. It is understandable that this constant pressure should have led to attempts on the part of various Israelite groups to constitute their own state and standing army to face their enemies.  This chapter is the story of how this "counterrevolutionary" tendency triumphed in the long run, and how it co-opted the notion of Yahweh's kingdom to serve as its own ideological justification.

It was probably in the early twelfth century that the Philistine sea peoples settled as a ruling caste in the five cities that dominated the southern coastal plain of the land of Canaan (Gath, Asdod, Gaza, Askelon, and Ekron). Their arrival coincided both with the retreat of Egyptian hegemony over Canaan and with the successful organization of the rebellious peasant groups into the tribal league called Israel. They quickly adopted the language and culture of Canaan. They had, however, two major military advantages that in the course of time led to the spread of their influence over most of the coastal plains and into the hill country where the Israelite tribes had established their dominance: the Philistines operated not as single city-states, but as a military coalition of tyrants *(seranim)*. And they came into the land with knowledge of the manufacture of iron implements.

This was the time of the transition in Canaan from the dominance of bronze technology to that of iron technology. But the transition was not an easy one. Iron tools were much superior to bronze ones. Their greater strength and durability were probably a factor in Israel's success in opening the hill country for cultivation. Iron plows could break soil where bronze was not efficient. Iron axes could clear brush and woods with less labor than bronze. Iron picks could carve cisterns and canals in the rock for irrigation.

And iron was also a formidable weapon when made into spears and swords and when used to rim the wheels of chariots.

But there was a problem. The manufacture of iron tools required a technique that was not easily mastered, and that made the trade of smiths a very valuable one. The Philistines introduced iron tools into Canaan. It seems that Israelite peasants were able to acquire the new and better tools, but that they did not acquire the techniques for making them. According to texts like 1 Sam. 13:19–23 the peasants had to go down to Philistine smiths even for the repair and sharpening of their iron tools. For obvious reasons, the peasants were not permitted to acquire iron weapons. This put Israel at a permanent technological inferiority with respect to the Philistines.[27]

Militarily, Israel was able to survive only because of the protection offered by the rugged terrain, where Philistine chariots were greatly reduced in their effectiveness. But as the Philistines tightened their control over the land of Canaan the Israelite organization in autonomous tribal units came to appear a weakness, and the desire grew for monarchy. The first attempt to establish a kingship in Israel of which we are informed was that of Abimelech of Shechem. His kingship was based on a Canaanite-Israelite coalition that probably had anti-Philistine intentions. His reign lasted only three years, however, and he was assassinated by his own subjects. There is no indication that his rule was widely recognized among the Israelite tribes or that he was able to mount an effective army.

We are better informed about the monarchy established by Saul of the central Israelite tribe of Benjamin. Saul first became known in Israel when he led the traditional militias of free men against the Ammonites and freed the city of Jabesh in Transjordan. In the wake of this military success, the leaders of the people anointed Saul king at the ancient Israelite sanctuary of Gilgal on the lower Jordan River (1 Sam. 11). The principal task of his rule was defense against the Philistines: "There was hard fighting against the Philistines all the days of Saul; and when Saul saw any strong man, or any valiant man, he attached him to himself" (1 Sam. 14:52). In spite of certain successes with his standing army of Israelites, Saul did not succeed in establishing a dynasty or a court. His failure was surely related to the ambiguity of making Israelite classless society the basis for a state.

It was David of the tribe of Judah who succeeded in founding a stable Israelite monarchy. His success was built first of all on the strength and loyalty of his army, and secondly on his ability to take up the strengths of the Israelite ideology and appeal to the loyalty it inspired for the novel purpose of supporting his kingship as the earthly representation of Yahweh's rule in Israel.

From the beginning David did not rely on the traditional Israelite army of free men. His army was made up of men who, for one reason or another, felt displaced by society. He built up this army in the mountains of Judah, where it acquired military experience in skirmishes with Saul's army and with the enemies of Judah. At this early stage his army is described thus:

> David departed from there and escaped to the cave of Adullam; and when his brothers and all his father's house heard it, they went down there to him. And every one who was in distress, and every one who was in debt, and every one who was discontented, gathered to him; and he became captain over them. And there were with him about four hundred men [1 Sam. 22:1–2].

Already at this early stage, before he was recognized by anybody as a king, David began to demand tribute from the inhabitants of Judah to support his army. The story of his dealings with Nabal illustrates his procedure. He expected a good share of the wool of this rich herdsman in return for the protection offered by his men (1 Sam. 25). David managed to take advantage of the regional sentiment of Judah to win for himself the protection of the populace in the face of the incursions of King Saul with the official army of the tribes of Israel.

When the army grew too large to live off the populace without creating resentment, David made a tactical retreat to the Philistine city of Gath, becoming the vassal of the feudal lord of the city with control over the town of Ziklag (1 Sam. 27). From the legitimacy that this arrangement offered him, David was able to consolidate his army with campaigns against towns that were the enemies of Judah as well as Gath, taking booty and sending a share of it to the elders of Judah (1 Sam. 30:26). By this means he won the support of his own tribe. When Saul was killed in combat with the Philistines, David was called to the city of Hebron and crowned the king of Judah (2 Sam. 2:1–4). There followed a struggle between the heirs of Saul and the men of David for the rule over Israel, ending with the victory of David and his proclamation as king by the elders of the tribes of Israel (2 Sam. 5:1–3).

David consecrated his success and consolidated his power by conquering the powerful city of Jerusalem, which had remained a Canaanite enclave between the territories controlled by the Israelite tribes of Judah and Benjamin. Because this city had never joined the Israelite movement, it was still a monarchy, with a long tradition as such. It was the only city in the hill country to preserve intact the Asiatic mode of production that the Israelite peasants had abolished elsewhere in the mountains. Therefore it did not form part of any of the tribes of Israel, and none of them had any sort of claim upon it. When David conquered it the city became a direct possession of the crown, in Canaanite fashion.[28] It came to be called the City of David (2 Sam. 5:6–10); and like every oriental despot David erected a palace as a symbol of his power (2 Sam. 5:11–12).

Our texts make it clear that there were many sectors, and not only in Judah, that greeted with pleasure the establishment of the monarchy. The powerful army of David promised an unaccustomed security in the face of Philistine incursions. And David was a pious worshipper of Yahweh, who went to great lengths to respect the traditions of Israel whose very material base he was subverting. With much pomp and ceremony he brought the ark of the covenant, symbol of Yahweh's throne, to a resting place in the City of David (2 Sam. 6; Ps. 132). He appointed as one of his two high priests Abiathar of Nŏb, who seems to have been related to the priestly family of the Yahweh temple at Shiloh which the Philistines destroyed (2 Sam. 8:17). He was remembered for many centuries to come as a composer of psalms to Yahweh.

But probably more important than his personal piety was the political organization of his kingdom, in which he appears to have done the utmost to preserve as much as possible of the traditional tribal system.[29] In addition to his personal army, commanded by Benaiah, David had a standing army made up of rotating contingents supplied by the tribes and commanded by Joab, his nephew (1 Chron. 7:1–15; 2 Sam. 8:15–18). In this manner, he was able to give the tribal structures a function within his kingdom. Important also was the conquest of foreign states: various Aramaean groups, Ammon, Edom, and Moab. This allowed him to support his army and the beginnings of a civilian bureaucracy without resorting to the taxation of free Israelites. The whole Israelite revolution had started in order to get away from such tribute, and surely its imposition would have caused unrest.

Even though David had problems in consolidating his kingship, he appears in our texts as a very able leader, who recognized the limits that Israelite tradition imposed and did no more than what was then possible. All in all, he provided the protection the tribes wanted from the Philistines at minimal cost to their economic and political freedoms, with the additional benefits of a small empire that allowed for some ostentation in their new capital city.

David's successor was his son Solomon, who did not have his father's sensitivity for Israelite values, while having a greater craving for the luxuries that oriental courts could offer. The royal bureaucracy increased phenomenally, to such an extent that taxation was broadened to include Israel:

Solomon ruled over all the kingdoms from the Euphrates to the land of the Philistines and to the border of Egypt; they brought tribute and served Solomon all the days of his life. Solomon's provision for one day was thirty cors of fine flour, and sixty cors of meal, ten fat oxen, and twenty pasture-fed cattle, a hundred sheep, besides harts, gazelles, roe-bucks and fatted fowl. . . . Solomon also had forty thousand stalls of horses for his chariots, and twelve thousand horsemen. The governors [of the twelve provinces into which he had divided Israel] supplied provision for King Solomon, and for all who came to his table, each one in his month; they let nothing be lacking. Barley also and straw for the horses and swift steeds they brought to the place where it was required, each ac-

cording to his charge [1 Kings 5:1–3, 6–8; Eng.
4:21–23; 26–28].

Solomon had established a state very much like the Canaanite states from which the Israelite tribes had withdrawn, only more so!

All of this betrayal of the Israelite revolution was con-
cealed beneath a luxurious show of devotion to Yahweh.
Solomon built a temple for the worship of Yahweh that
could compete with the monuments of the great empires of
the Near East in its glory. For its construction cedars were
brought from Lebanon, bronze from the mines of Ezion-
Geber, and gold from still more distant places, not to mention the quarried stone from the mountains of Judah itself
(1 Kings 6). But these impressive works do not happen by
themselves. The labor required was partly salaried and
partly forced labor, partly from conquered peoples and
partly from the Israelite tribes themselves:

> King Solomon raised a levy of forced labor out of all
> Israel; and the levy numbered thirty thousand men.
> And he sent them to Lebanon, ten thousand a month
> in relays; they would be a month in Lebanon and two
> months at home; Adoniram was in charge of the levy.
> Solomon also had seventy thousand burden-bearers
> and eighty thousand hewers of stone in the hill country
> [1 Kings 5:27–29; Eng. 5:13–15].

Besides the building of the temple there were other works
of construction in Jerusalem to give the capital an appropri-
ate atmosphere of luxury for the new Israelite court (1
Kings 7).

This was exactly the kind of labor which the Egyptian
Pharaoh had imposed on the people of Yahweh and by reason of which Moses had led them to freedom in the desert.

The tributes and the forced labors were much worse than those that had inspired their forebears to rebel against the Canaanite kings who oppressed them. It is hardly surprising that the Israelite tribes rose in rebellion against this oriental despotism that Solomon had imposed with such ostentation. Jeroboam the son of Nebat, an Ephraimite who was in charge of the work crews from his tribe, was urged to rebel by a prophet of Yahweh, Ahijah of Shilo (1 Kings 11:26–40). The revolt was unsuccessful and Jeroboam went into exile in Egypt. But on the occasion of Solomon's death Jeroboam returned to lead a successful secession of the bulk of the tribes from the rule of Solomon's heir, his son Rehoboam:

> And Solomon slept with his fathers, and was buried in the city of David his father; and Rehoboam his son reigned in his stead. Rehoboam went to Shechem, for all Israel had come to Shechem to make him king. And when Jeroboam the son of Nebat heard of it (for he was still in Egypt, whither he had fled from King Solomon), then Jeroboam returned from Egypt. And they sent and called him; and Jeroboam and all the assembly of Israel came and said to Rehoboam, "Your father made our yoke heavy. Now therefore lighten the hard service of your father and his heavy yoke upon us, and we will serve you.". . . The king did not hearken to the people. . . . When all Israel heard that Jeroboam had returned, they sent and called him to the assembly and made him king over all Israel. There was none that followed the house of David, but the tribe of Judah only [1 Kings 11:43; 12:1–4, 15, 20].

In the name of Yahweh, the tribes of Israel thus shook off the oppression of Solomon, who had made them labor to

build Yahweh's temple. The Davidic dynasty was reduced
from its imperial dimensions to those of an ordinary Canaanite state, a little larger than the others but smaller than
the bulk of Israel that joined the revolt. In that reduced
condition it survived for four hundred years.

We have seen that the main support of the Davidic state
was the strength of a professional army, which was used at
first against the enemies of Israel, but which in the second
generation was used to back the heavy tributes exacted from
Israel in goods and in labor. Solomon did not neglect the
other support of David's kingship, his appeal to the Yahweh
faith. In his own way, he developed the doctrine of
Yahweh's kingship even more than his father. His construction of the temple was an impressive attempt to make
Yahweh the liberator into Yahweh the patron of David's
dynasty. The Psalms, most of which were composed for use
in this temple, give direct testimony to the manner in which
Yahweh was there worshipped. We can properly speak of a
royal ideology. One of the cornerstones of this ideological
elaboration is the doctrine of Yahweh's covenant with
Israel, appropriately modified to fit the new circumstances:

> I have made a covenant with my chosen one,
> I have sworn to David my servant:
> "I will establish your descendants for ever,
> and build your throne for all generations."
> He shall cry to me, "Thou art my father,
> my God and the rock of my salvation."
> And I will make him the first-born,
> the highest of the kings of the earth.
> I will not violate my covenant,
> or alter the word that went forth from my lips.
> Once for all I have sworn by my holiness;
> I will not lie to David.

His line shall endure for ever,
his throne as long as the sun before me
[Ps. 89:3-4, 26-28, 35-36].

Yahweh's covenant with Israel had been the constitution
that had ordered the life of the Israelite tribes for over two
centuries. It had laid the foundation for Yahweh's kingdom.
Now the spokesmen of the new temple had made of that
covenant the justification for monarchy. The partners of
the original covenant were Yahweh and the people of Israel.
This new covenant, it is said in the Psalms, was made between Yahweh and David. The stipulations of the original
covenant were the conditions that Yahweh imposed on his
people, the most important being exclusive loyalty to
Yahweh, who had liberated them and was the guarantee of
their continued liberty. In this royal version of the covenant, Yahweh imposed conditions on himself, namely,
eternal and exclusive loyalty to David and his descendants!
If the descendants of David should rebel against Yahweh,
God promised that in his punishment he would never sus-
pend the eternal covenant made with them (Ps. 89:31-34).
The Davidic dynasty was given, so to speak, carte blanche
from the king of the universe.

Upon this foundation of Yahweh's covenant with David,
court intellectuals built a whole structure of royal ideology
with elements largely borrowed from other royal establish-
ments of the region. One of the elements of the royal ideology was the doctrine that the king was the son of Yahweh,
an adoptive son to be sure, but a son nonetheless:

I will tell the decree of Yahweh.
He said to me: "You are my son,
today I have begotten you.
Ask of me, and I will make the nations your heritage,

and the ends of the earth your possession.
You shall break them with a rod of iron,
and dash them in pieces like a potter's vessel"

[Ps.2:7–9].

The king of Egypt was proclaimed a god and the son of
god. In Babylon it was taught that the king was the son of a
goddess. But it was against this kind of theology and its
political consequences that Israel had accepted in its covenant with Yahweh the first commandment forbidding worship of gods who were not liberators.

According to another psalm, Yahweh shall invite the new
king to sit at his side and declare him a priest according to
the order of Melchizedek (Ps. 110:1, 4). Now Melchizedek
was a legendary priest-king of pre-Israelite Jerusalem.

A royal wedding psalm carries this tendency so far as to
call the king God himself (Ps. 45:6). And a prayer for the
king expresses the idea, common in antiquity, that the fertil-
ity of the fields and the fecundity of the flocks are bound up
with the special powers of the king (Ps. 72:6, "May he be
like rain that falls on the mown grass, like showers that water the earth").

The Jerusalem temple and its personnel had an important
impact, not only on the way life was lived for ordinary
Israelite working people, but also on the information that
has reached us about Israel. Almost all of our knowledge of
Israel has passed through the filter of the ideological work
of the Jerusalem priests and scribes. For this reason it has
become difficult for later generations to perceive the significance of the early Israelite project of realizing Yahweh's
kingdom. The fact that the Davidic kingship was a betrayal
of that project has also been obscured by the redactional
activity of the Jerusalem scribes. The royal ideology domi-
nates a good part of the books of the Bible.

It seems likely that in the kingdom of Israel (the Northern Kingdom) the egalitarian traditions of tribal Israel were preserved more faithfully than in the south. For one thing, there was never a stable dynasty to secure itself and impose its imprint on the religious traditions. Uprisings and military coups were frequent. For another the political scene was affected by a series of prophets of Yahweh. A prophetic figure like Elisha was able, in the name of Yahweh, to incite a rebellion that overthrew the Omri dynasty (2 Kings 9). In other words, the conflict between royalty and the egalitarian traditions of tribal Israel persisted for several centuries in northern Israel. But this kingdom was one of the casualties of the expansion of Assyrian imperialism in the late eighth century. Some of the Israelite Levites escaped to Judah and their presence was no doubt one of the factors in the revival of Israelite traditions there in the late seventh century.

In some ways the reform movement associated with King Josiah in late seventh-century Judah was a return to the Yahwistic tradition of Israel's origins. However, a negative result of this reform was the imposition of a temple monopoly over the cultural life of the nation. All of the lesser sanctuaries were destroyed in the attempt to wipe out impurities (2 Kings 23). As a result, it was the priests and scribes of the Jerusalem temple, often servile to the interests of the court, who prepared the texts by which we know of Israel and the faith in Yahweh its God. Quite naturally, David and his dynasty came through in the texts as more faithful Yahwists than they seem to us today.

In spite of the subversion by the Davidic line of Israel's revolutionary project of a classless society, all was not lost. If the idea of Yahweh's kingdom was to fulfill its function of legitimizing the exploitation of working people, it had to preserve elements that proclaimed justice and the defense of

society's victims. As any ideology must do, this one masked
the reality of a class society in which the court lived in relative luxury from the labors of village people. This was done
by presenting the king as the defender of the oppressed persons of Israel, appointed by Yahweh to look out for the
interests of the poor. The kingdom of God, with its egalitarian content, served to conceal a different reality. To make it
credible, this ideology, like all ideologies, had a utopian horizon.[30] But the existence of this horizon also exposed the
system to possible attacks from within the legitimacy of the
official theology. In this manner, Absalom, the rebellious
son of David, was able to take advantage of his father's
negligence in responding to the petitions of the people to
present himself as a better defender of the victims of injustice than his father. By this means he won popular support
for his rebellion (2 Sam. 15:1-6). The appeal of Absalom
was possible because of the doctrine that the king was the
great defender of the humble, as in Psalm 72:

> Give the king thy justice, Yahweh,
> and thy righteousness to the king's son!
> May he judge thy people with righteousness,
> and thy poor with justice.
> Let the mountains bear prosperity for the people,
> and the hills righteousness!
> May he defend the cause of the poor of the people,
> give deliverance to the needy,
> and crush the oppressor!
> Let him deliver the needy when he calls,
> the poor and him who has no helper.
> Let him take pity on the weak and the needy,
> and save the lives of the poor [Ps. 72:1-4, 12-13].[31]

More importantly, this utopian horizon of the official
theology of Jerusalem served as the basis for the preaching

of the great Jerusalem prophet Isaiah. Isaiah accepted the basic elements of the Jerusalem theology. He believed that God had chosen David and his descendants to reign forever. He believed that Jerusalem was a city chosen by God for his resting place. But he also took seriously the affirmations of that theology with regard to Yahweh and the king as the defenders of the defenseless, and in his preaching the utopian horizon of the royal ideology was brought near enough to shine on the exploitation it was designed to cover. Isaiah denounced a rich and pious cult practiced zealously by a people indifferent to the fate of the weak in their exploitation (Isa. 1:10–17). Officially Jerusalem was proclaimed to be the holy city—but Isaiah saw that its political and religious leaders had converted it into a center of crime against working people:

> How the faithful city has become a harlot,
> she that was full of justice!
> Righteousness lodged in her,
> but now murderers.
> Your silver has become dross,
> your wine mixed with water.
> Your princes are rebels and companions of thieves.
> Everyone loves a bribe,
> and runs after gifts.
> They do not defend the fatherless,
> and the widow's cause does not come to them.
> Therefore, the oracle of the Lord Yahweh Sebaot,
>   the Mighty One of Israel:
> "Ah, I will vent my wrath on my enemies,
> and avenge myself of my foes.
> I will turn my hand against you
> and will smelt away your dross as with lye
> and remove all your slag.
> And I will restore your judges as at the first,

and your counselors as at the beginning.
Afterward you shall be called the city of righteousness,
the faithful city" [Isa. 1:21–26].

Isaiah did not announce the destruction of Jerusalem. He
was no radical like Amos. Staying within the Jerusalem
royal theology, he announced a purification of the holy city
like the purification of metal to remove impurities, after
which the city would truly be a city of righteousness, as the
cult practitioners said it was.

The prophet could see that the kings no longer wanted to
listen to the word of Yahweh (Isa. 7:10–13). State bureau-
crats made decrees and verdicts that trampled on the rights
of the poor (Isa. 10:1–4). Userers and merchants were seiz-
ing the lands of peasants (Isa. 5:8–10). But Yahweh, according to the official theology, had founded Mount Zion as a
refuge for the poor (Ps. 132:13–15; Isa. 14:28–32).

Faced with this contradiction between the utopian ideals
of the official cult and the brutal facts of material existence,
Isaiah announced that Yahweh would cut down Jerusalem
with its royal house as a forest is cut down (Isa. 6:10–13;
10:32–34). Nothing would be left but tree trunks. And yet,
Yahweh, faithful to his covenant with David (which Isaiah
seems never to have questioned), would make of that trunk
a holy seed (Isa. 6:13) and would draw from it a branch for
Jesse (Isa. 11:1). This new royal lineage would come forth
after the punishment of the current kings and would make
real the justice for which Yahweh had anointed David:

There shall come forth a shoot from the stump of Jesse
    [David's father]
and a branch shall grow out of his roots.
And the Spirit of Yahweh shall rest upon him,
the spirit of wisdom and understanding,

the spirit of counsel and might,
the spirit of knowledge and the fear of Yahweh.
He will not judge by what his eyes see,
or decide by what his ears hear;
but with righteousness he shall judge the poor
and decide with equity for the meek of the earth;
and he shall smite the earth with the rod of his mouth,
and with the breath of his lips he shall slay the wicked
[Isa. 11:1–4].

Thus Isaiah built on the royal theology a hope for the coming of a true and just king, the Messiah. This hope is developed in oracles found in Isaiah 9:1–6; 32:1–5, 15–20; and 2:1–5. In these prophecies Isaiah relied on the official declarations that Yahweh would punish the children of David who rebelled against his statutes (Ps. 89:31–34; 2 Sam. 7:14–15), but would not reject his eternal covenant with David nor utterly destroy his dynasty. With respect to the promises concerning Jerusalem, Isaiah's prophecies are analogous. So that peace might come as announced in the cult, and so that Jerusalem might be a refuge for the weak, it would first have to be uprooted and there would have to come forth another king chosen by Yahweh (from David's lineage) and other priests who would serve him faithfully on the holy hill.

Let us sum up our investigation up to this point. In the thirteenth century B.C. there emerged in Canaan an attempt on the part of various peasant groups moved by the spirit of liberty, the aspiration for a classless society. These rebellious groups gathered together into various tribes under the banner of Yahweh, the God who led Moses and his followers out of their oppression in Egypt. For over two centuries Israel existed as Yahweh's kingdom, fighting off constant attempts of the surrounding states to subdue them anew. Then, under the fierce pressure of the culturally more advanced Philistines, Israel chose a king for itself. David succeeded in founding an enduring army and state with minimal clash with the antistatist traditions of Israel. However, in succeeding generations the royal court and the Jerusalem temple became the creators of a theological justification for domination even superior to the Baal cults of the previous Canaanite overlords. Thus did Yahweh's kingdom become an ideology of domination. Against this betrayal of the original historical project of the Israelite peasants, prophetic voices were raised in the name of Yahweh. Outstanding among these was Isaiah of Jerusalem.

4

God's Kingdom as Hierocratic Society

With the destruction of Jerusalem and the deportation of the royal court in the early sixth century B.C., the Davidic monarchy came to an end. With the end of Israelite monarchy, the royal ideology that served to undergird it came to an end also.

It was not the end of Israel as Yahweh's people, however. The transition to the new form under which Israel continued was prepared unwittingly by the great reform movement under King Josiah (640–609 B.C.). The central reform implemented by Josiah in his attempt to restore Israel to its former greatness was a strong centralization of all the national life around Jerusalem. Part of this centralization was the destruction of all the religious sanctuaries in the country with the exception of the Jerusalem temple. This gave the Zadokite priests who officiated there a monopoly on legitimate religious practice in Israel. It was they who were to direct the Israelite historical project when "normal" life resumed several generations later.

Along with the rest of the city of Jerusalem, the temple was also destroyed by the Babylonian armies in the year 587

B.C. The royal officials and the priests were sent to Babylon into exile. In other words, the entire ruling class was deported. The Babylonians left the peasants in their villages. It is likely that life did not change much for them. It is characteristic of societies with "Asiatic" social structures that only the state makes history. The producers in the villages contribute their labor but have little influence on the historical actions of society. Because the ruling class does not participate economically in the productive process, their disappearance or replacement does not shake the structure of village life, which, as we saw, is organized along kinship lines. It is probable that the disruption at the village level was not great. Of course, tribute now had to be paid to Babylonian governors, but this probably was little different in quantity from the tribute formerly rendered to the court of Judah. We do not know how the peasants responded to their situation in the absence of the Davidic court and the temple at Jerusalem.

We do know much more about the Jewish community in exile in Babylon. Here the priests prepared their return. They planned the reconstruction of the temple and the recapture of their place of privilege within society. It is these projects that now concern us.

It was among the exiles in Babylon that the priestly document (P) of the Pentateuch was written. This was a revisionist history of Israel's antecedents in creation, patriarchal wanderings, exodus, wilderness wanderings, and the occupation of the land of Canaan. According to P, God made his covenant with Abraham, the first patriarch of Israel (Gen. 17). It is striking to look at this covenant because of its resemblance to the royal version of the covenant. God declares that he has chosen Abraham and his descendants forever as his people. The concrete meaning of this eternal choice is twofold: Abraham's descendants will multiply greatly so that many nations come from them, and God will give them "all the land of Canaan." The only obligation that the covenant imposes on Abraham is the circumcision of all the males born into his family as a sign of their being chosen by God. The obvious resemblance to the royal covenant suggests that it—not Sinai—was the priestly model.

The exodus becomes in P's reworking of it first of all the occasion for God to multiply his signs and wonders for the marvel of future generations. The Sinai pericope is not so much the occasion of the revelation of the laws to guide Israel's life and the establishing of a covenant with the people as it is the revelation of the whole apparatus of worship by means of which the people shall be able to lead a pure life in Yahweh's land (Exod. 25–31; 35–40). The main purpose of Israel's life is to praise God by means of their pure and religious life. They have no need of a king. They do need properly ordained priests to maintain the purity of their worship.

P was not the only program of restoration worked out in the Babylonian exile. Ezekiel or his spiritual heirs were responsible for a similar project, the program which is preserved in the book of Ezekiel, chapters 40 to 48. A new temple stands in the center of reconstructed Israel in this design. The design itself is largely devoted to describing the geographical arrangements for priests (Zadokites only), Levites, the prince and his court, and the eleven remaining tribes. The objective of their distribution is to preserve the temple from defilement. The priests and Levites are to live in the area immediately adjacent to the temple grounds, and the city of Jerusalem and the prince is to occupy the next spaces (Ezek. 45:1–12). This corresponds to their level in the hierarchy that the design envisions. The Zadokite priests are the only ones permitted to officiate at the sacri-

fices in the temple. The Levites are allowed to participate in
the temple service but have no right to officiate in the sacrifices. The prince's primary function is to provide the animals required for the sacrifices.

Both Ezekiel and P therefore elaborated models for a
hierocratic society, that is, one in which authority resides in
the priestly caste. It was this general model that guided the
reconstruction of Judah under the auspices of the Persian
Empire. In the year 538 B.C. the Persian troops entered the
city of Babylon and took over the center of power, displac-
ing the Babylonians from command over their empire. One
of the measures of the Persian emperor Cyrus that year was
an edict authorizing the restoration of the temple and the
city of Jerusalem:

> Thus says Cyrus king of Persia: "Yahweh, the God of
> heaven, has given me all the kingdoms of the earth,
> and he has charged me to build him a house at Jerusa-
> lem, which is in Judah. Whoever is among you of all
> his people, may his God be with him, and let him go up
> to Jerusalem, which is in Judah, and rebuild the house
> of Yahweh, the God of Israel—he is the God who is in
> Jerusalem; and let each survivor, in whatever place he
> sojourns, be assisted by the men of his place with silver
> and gold, with goods and with beasts, besides freewill
> offerings for the house of God which is in Jerusalem"
> [Ezra 1:2–4].

At first sight it seems strange that a Persian king should
help in the restoration of the worship of Yahweh in Jerusalem. It was, however, Persian policy to sponsor the religious
centers and the priestly castes of the peoples they conquered. In line with this policy, when Cyrus entered Babylon he became the restorer of the worship of Marduk and of
the privileges of the Marduk priests.[32]

The support of the priestly caste in Jerusalem was a considered policy. A century later Artaxerxes followed the same design of imperial rule when he sent Ezra to impose "the law of God" on the people of Judah (Ezra 7:11–20). This edict of Artaxerxes authorized Ezra to take money from the official treasury for the needs of the restoration of the cult entrusted to him. It also granted an exemption from taxes to "the priests, Levites, cantors, doorkeepers, temple servants, or other servants of this house of God" (Ezra 7:24).

Persian policy was to impose upon the village productive base of Judah a priestly class that would serve as a buffer between the producers and the final oppressor (the imperial authorities). From the viewpoint of Judah's internal life it meant taking up again Josiah's project of centering the national life on the temple. This time, however, the temple was backed by the political power, not of a Judean monarchy, but of the Persian crown. The historical fact was that the Persian Empire supported the exile community in putting into practice the project they had worked out in Babylon.

Within this hierocratic society Yahweh's kingdom took on certain characteristic forms. During the reign of the Persian king Darius, the building of the temple was undertaken with great enthusiasm. At the time, the governor of Judah was a native Judean appointed by the Persians, a certain Zerubbabel. About his person messianic hopes sprang up, reviving the prophet Isaiah's promises. Haggai, a prophet whose principal role was the encouragement of the builders of the temple, announced that Zerubbabel had been chosen by Yahweh to destroy the power of the nations:

Speak to Zerubbabel, governor of Judah, saying, I am about to shake the heavens and the earth, and to overthrow the throne of kingdoms; I am about to destroy the strength of the kingdoms of the nations, and over-

throw the chariots and their riders; and the horses and
their riders shall go down, every one by the sword of
his fellow. On that day, says Yahweh Sebaot, I will take
you, O Zerubbabel my servant, the son of Shealtiel,
says Yahweh, and make you like a signet ring; for I
have chosen you, says Yahweh Sebaot [Hag. 2:21–23].

For Haggai, Persian rule was provisional. Once the temple
was in place Yahweh would take the governor and use him
to establish his kingdom around that temple.

A contemporary prophet, Zechariah, announced the ad-
vent of Yahweh's kingdom under two messiahs (anointed
ones), the high priest Joshua and Zerubbabel the governor
(Zech. 4:1–14). In this kingdom, Yahweh would establish
the temple as his place on earth and would make the priests
separated for its service his agents. The governor would ob-
viously be secondary in the whole scheme.

The substance of the priestly historical project came to
pass, although Persian rule remained a constant. The
priestly class adjusted to this fact with little difficulty. The
temple became the one thing necessary to consolidate their
domination.

But this hierocratic project was not the only one worked
out in the black years of exile that followed the destruction
of Jerusalem. Among the exiles there arose a prophet who
spoke on behalf of the popular classes with a different vision of what Yahweh's kingdom meant for their times. We
refer to Deutero-Isaiah, the anonymous author of the prophetic sayings collected in the book of Isaiah, chapters 40 to
55.[33] In beautiful words of encouragement for the people he
announced:

How beautiful upon the mountains
are the feet of him who brings good tidings,

who publishes peace, who brings good tidings of good,
who publishes salvation,
who says to Zion, "Your God reigns" [Isa. 52:7].

His language is lyrical, designed more to encourage a desperate people than to instruct them. For that reason it is not possible to put together as many details of this project as those so amply drawn by Ezekiel for the priestly project. It is certainly significant that nothing is said of priests or of the sacrificial cult. The prophet does mention in 44:28 that the temple will be rebuilt as part of the general reconstruction, but gives the fact no real prominence. For our purposes, the most important element of his vision is what he has to say about the covenant. Deutero-Isaiah moves in the tradition of Isaiah, and so it is that his theology is that of the covenant with David. Notwithstanding, in Isaiah 55:1–5 he announces that "the everlasting covenant, the steadfast promises to David" are to be fulfilled in the entire people, who will become the instructor of the nations of the earth. This prophet does not wish for a restoration of the Davidic monarchy.[34] He expects rather that Yahweh will place Cyrus the Persian at the political top of the world (Isa. 45:1–7). But the rulership of the nations is not to be exerted from the top, but from the gentle persuasion of the truth by God's servant Israel (Isa. 42:1–4). Israel is to become "a light to the nations" (Isa. 49:6).

The restoration was (unfortunately) a project of the priests and not of the people, who must have listened hopefully to Deutero-Isaiah. The popular project of Deutero-Isaiah was kept alive with some difficulty under priestly domination. It continued to produce prophetic spokespersons, none of them known to us by name. Their sayings have been collected in chapters 56 to 66 of the book of Isaiah. The influence of Deutero-Isaiah in these prophecies from the restoration is quite marked. Chapters 60 to 62 preserve some prophetic songs celebrating the reconstruction of Jerusalem with not a word about the temple. Chapter 58 is a strong attack on the fasting that was such a prominent part of the religion of the restoration period and that, according to the prophet, masked the exploitation of the workers and "punches for the destitute" (Isa. 58:3–4). The "new heavens and new earth" that are announced in Isaiah 65:17–25 have houses and vineyards but there is not a word about any temple. And the oracle in Isaiah 66:1–2 makes a frontal attack on the project dearest to the priests:

> Thus says Yahweh:
> "Heaven is my throne
> and the earth is my footstool;
> what is the house which you would build for me,
> and what is the place of my rest?
> All these things my hand has made,
> and so all these things are mine, says Yahweh.
> But this is the man to whom I will look,
> he that is humble and contrite in spirit,
> and trembles at my word."

It is hard not to read here evidence for a clash of the project of the priests and the project of the people. Each had its prophetic spokespersons, Haggai and Zechariah on one side and the unnamed prophets of Isaiah 56–66 on the other.

In Deutero-Isaiah and his successors we find defenders of the people, the workers who toiled on the land. Here we find the hope for Yahweh's kingdom, a society that would not be class-oriented or hierocratic.[35] In the face of imperial support for the priestly project this other one never reached historical fulfilment and these prophetic voices were eventually silenced. Yahweh's rule was expressed through the temple and the many regulations for holiness administered by the priests, with the blessing of the Persian and later the Hellenistic authorities.

In the new theology Yahweh became first of all a creator, the creator of the universe, who chose among all the peoples of the earth Abraham and his descendants to reveal his commandments and to commend to them the place of his dwelling. Sinai was transformed from the place where a free people was constituted to the place where God revealed the ordinances for his legitimate worship.

5

God's Kingdom in
First-Century Palestine

In our investigation of the kingdom of God within the Bible, this chapter is second in importance only to that on the origins of Israel (chapter 2). This is so because the historical project of God's kingdom of which the primitive Jesus movement was the bearer survived the debacle of the Jewish-Roman War to inspire the Christian religion that was to become the religion of Europe. Our entire study is based on the open question whether or not that Christian religion can be considered good news for the poor. By thus stressing the importance of the Jesus movement because of its seminal character for Christian religion we are recognizing a historical fact, not judging it. The judgment must be made if the poor are to achieve salvation, but a biblical scholar is not the one to make it. The decision whether the Christian faith offers hope for the poor must be made by the poor themselves. Nevertheless political decisions are not made without taking into account the realities of history, and Christianity is a historical reality to be dealt with, for good or for ill. And so, regardless of where we Latin American Christians come out in our political evaluation of

the Christian message, the fact of the Jesus movement is a major historical reality with which we must deal.[36]

In this unit of our study what is most important, the Jesus movement in its origins, must remain largely hypothetical. About Jesus and his Galilean movement, about their strategy to bring about God's kingdom, we are informed only through the documents of a Christian church already uprooted from the Palestinian context in which it was born. That our investigation on this point is hypothetical does not mean that it is not serious or that it does not merit scientific respect. It will merit this respect to the extent that it does justice to the sources and succeeds in explaining the facts for which we have trustworthy documents. A good hypothesis will then be confirmed or disconfirmed by the research it inspires on the documents.

It is not very difficult to establish the main outlines of the historical situation of Palestine in the first century of the Christian Era. The various Jewish movements inspired by the expectation of God's kingdom were so many attempts to answer the challenges of that situation. Any hypothesis about the Jesus movement must rest on our knowledge of that situation, and then take seriously the subsequent Christian texts that come mostly from outside of Palestine. If it does so, it will not be just another projection of our desires like that profusion of biographies of Jesus that liberal idealism has produced for two centuries.[37]

We have divided our study of the first century into two parts. In this first part we shall deal with Palestinian movements guided by the prophetic promises of the coming kingdom. Among these we shall emphasize the Jesus movement, because it is so seminal to our identity as Christians.[38] In a second part we shall focus on the Christian communities scattered over the Greco-Roman world outside of Palestine.

Palestine under the Roman Empire. According to historical materialism, the introduction of private property launched humankind on the irreversible path of making history. The irreversible character of the history thus launched has to do with the destruction of the "natural" productive community, the peasant village. Once the village structure was broken up, there was no turning back. Empirically, civilization began with the introduction of a tributary mode of production in places like Egypt, Mesopotamia, Mexico, and China. But in these societies the state was superimposed on the village, and village structures persisted. It was the survival of the village that made possible the Israelite antistatist revolution, which was a more "primitive" society than the Canaanite society it replaced. The break-up of village structures only occurred through the introduction of private property, especially over land. Private property was first made possible by the introduction of slave labor. And the Roman Empire was the greatest historical experiment in building a society on slave labor.[39]

The original accumulation of wealth in the city of Rome was achieved by means of its commercial enterprises. To protect its commercial interests Rome built a powerful army made up of the sons of the free peasants under its sphere of influence. Slaves were introduced to work the lands, which passed from the hands of villagers into those of wealthy nobles. Rome soon discovered that the cheapest way to acquire slaves was through war. Because slaves did not reproduce themselves in captivity at a sufficient rate to maintain the level of production desired, Rome was pushed to ever greater militarism and expansionism. By the first century of the Christian Era it had achieved its maximum extension.

In the course of its expansion, the Roman legions also conquered Palestine. It was Pompey who led the legions into Palestine in 63 B.C. Palestine was incorporated into the province of Syria, which was governed by a Roman proconsul. To a Hasmonean (the Jewish dynasty descended from the Maccabees) was entrusted the high priesthood, without administrative authority. The levying of tribute remained in the hands of the Syrian proconsul.

The mere presence of Roman authorities in Palestine did not overnight transform the character of Palestinian society. As we have seen, that society was organized according to an Asiatic mode of production. In the place of a royal court, the power of tribute over the productive villages rested in the hands of the temple personnel. Much remains to be done to understand how the tributary Palestinian society was meshed into the slave-based Roman Empire. It is clear, nevertheless, that slave production did not become the norm in Palestine. Cities were built on the Greco-Roman model, but they seem to have been enclaves within a society where traditional village life continued, and where the temple continued to play the role of the dominant class, it being in turn dominated by Roman military authorities. The interplay between these two types of class societies was basic for any strategy of popular liberation, and helps account for the various strategies we shall be examining. Not only is it difficult for us in the twentieth century to understand the interaction of these two class systems and their relative importance, those who struggled for liberation in the first century also differed in their interpretations of the reality of oppression they were experiencing. We shall return to this.

A further complicating factor was the rise of a local king, Herod the Idumean. Herod, whom Jews suspected of being a Jew only by convenience, was able through gaining the confidence of the Roman authorities to be recognized by the Senate in 40 B.C. as king with a good measure of auton-

omy. The Kingdom of Judea was separated from Syria and
came to depend directly on Caesar. In exchange for his autonomy Herod gave military protection to this flank of the
empire. During his reign (40–4 B.C.) Herod extracted an as-
tonishing amount of wealth from the people of Palestine, as
shown by the impressive buildings erected in Jerusalem and
in the new city of Caesarea. His was a reign of terror and
force, very effective principally through his good relations
with Rome. He also understood Palestinian society, and became the principal sponsor of the temple. His extensive
works of construction on the temple gave him a certain ve-
neer of legitimacy in the eyes of the Jews.

This superimposition of a slave empire on the back of a
tributary society worked very well during Herod's time, at
the cost of considerable sacrifice by the working population. But ten years after Herod's death, A.D. 6, Judea was
made a Roman province with its own proconsul who re-
sided in Caesarea. Galilee meanwhile remained a semi-
autonomous tetrarchy under the rule of a son of Herod
(Herod Antipas). It was a highly unstable situation.

For the next century Palestine was one of the constant
trouble spots of the empire. To understand this we must
remember again that this tributary system centered in the
temple. For six centuries the priestly class had been the ruling class. The religious ideology, with its symbolic center in
the temple, was the principal justification for and concealment of class domination in Palestine since the reform of
Josiah. During most of this time Palestine was under foreign domination. The extraction of surplus labor was carried out peacefully as long as the imperial authorities recognized the special characteristics of this society and allowed
the temple its dominant role in the control and exploitation
of the villagers. Difficulties arose only when the foreign
rulers tried to alter this system by imposing cities in the Hel-

lenistic style, with slavery and private property, and displaced Jerusalem and the temple from the center.

All social classes would see an attack on the temple as a threat, and its displacement from its privileged place would bring all classes together in opposition. This is what occurred when Antiochus Epiphanes tried to impose a Hellenistic social system on Palestine in the early second century B.C. Led by Judas Maccabeus and his successors, the Jews united in rebellion against the defiler of their temple. The situation in the first century of the Christian Era was a similar one. Roman toleration for Palestinian ways was never secure, and latent opposition would break into open rebellion when a Roman emperor or procurator overstepped the bounds established by long custom.

The Maccabean revolt in the second century B.C. had led to the establishment of a semi-autonomous kingdom in Jerusalem with a dynasty that combined royal and priestly functions with the awkward but necessary support of the Seleucid kings. This foreign support, plus the fact that the Hasmoneans were high priests without belonging to the Zadokite family, took away legitimacy from the regime and began a process of secularization that continued into the century that concerns us.

There were several strategies for coping with the threat to the social fabric both from without and from within. The Essenes were a sect with deep concern for the purity of the temple, which they believed was defiled by an unworthy priesthood. In the hope that the future held a purification of the same and a restoration of legitimate worship, in the meantime they withdrew from national life and from any participation in the temple. They lived in separate communities, studied the Scriptures, and prepared themselves for the coming of God's kingdom.

The Sadducees were the party that supported the official

arrangement of things and accepted the need for accommodating to the foreign authorities. They had their base in
Jerusalem in the priestly aristocracy. Except for the most
extreme situations, they always favored looking for a nego-
tiated settlement with the ruling Romans.

The Pharisees focused on the need for fulfilling the law of
Moses as the most important requirement of national life.
They had their base among the villages, and were strong in
Galilee. They were the direct religious leaders and teachers
in the synagogues of the villages where the people gathered
to learn their duties. They expressed the sentiments of the
majority. Theirs was a central role in the struggles with the
Romans. In ordinary circumstances they favored a policy
of peace with the rulers and awaiting God's action on
Israel's behalf. But each time that an emperor or a proconsul threatened to contaminate the temple or to prevent the
exercise of obedience to the law they threw their influence
against him and joined movements of rebellion.

Under Herod there was a situation of social calm, in spite
of the intensity of the exploitation. He seems to have understood the system. He kept the temple in opulent style. It was
with the incorporation of Judea as a province under a Roman procurator that the problems began that agitated
Palestine until the destruction of Jerusalem A.D. 70.

A new "sect" arose, that of the Zealots. This movement
was begun by Judas "the Galilean," who, at the time of the
census of Cirenius, which occurred at the same time as the
establishment of the province (A.D. 6), took up arms rather
than pay tribute to the Romans.[40] The theological basis for
their refusal to pay tribute was that by this action they
would be recognizing a human ruler alongside God (Josephus, *War* II. 118, 433). If God was to be king, there could
be no human king alongside him, not even a Jewish one.
They revived the tradition of armed struggle against foreign

domination that came from the Maccabees. But they were different in that they rejected monarchy. Theirs was a classic biblical position, reminiscent of that of Gideon. The difference was that they acknowledged the place of privilege of the temple, and therefore of the hierocratic class society.

The guerrilla movement that they carried on in the Galilean hills had its moments of importance. When the Emperor Caligula ordered that his statue be mounted in the temple (A.D. 40) the people joined them in readiness for armed rebellion. Caligula was assassinated before carrying out his intentions, and calm was restored to Palestine. The Zealots were again to play a dominant role when the entire people united in a war to restore the autonomy of the temple A.D. 66. Menachem, a descendant of Judas, was the chief of operations in Jerusalem in that year (Josephus, *War* II. 433ff. and VII. 320ff.).

The Jesus Movement and the Kingdom of God. With this background we are prepared to ask about the good news that Jesus and his followers had to offer to the villagers of Galilee. Luke summarizes Jesus' mission by having him quote from the book of Isaiah in his first public appearance in Galilee:

> The Spirit of the Lord is upon me,
> because he has anointed me to preach good news
>   to the poor.
> He has sent me to proclaim release to the captives
> and recovery of sight to the blind,
> to set at liberty those who are oppressed,
> to proclaim the acceptable year of the Lord
>   [Luke 4:18–19].

With this quotation Luke summarizes for his readers, most of whom presumably were not residents of Palestine, what was meant by preaching the kingdom of God. Mark does the same thing with a summary of Jesus' preaching of the gospel of God: "The time is fulfilled, and the kingdom of God is at hand; repent, and believe in the gospel" (Mark 1:15).

We are not interested here in Jesus' "messianic consciousness" or in his private understandings. Many generations of research in these themes have led to contradictory results. Our interest is focused instead on the historical project borne by Jesus and his Galilean movement, as it is told in the gospel narratives (from which we try to strip the overlay of theological justification for Jesus' death, see Fernando Belo, *A Materialist Reading of the Gospel of Mark* [Maryknoll, N.Y.: Orbis Books, 1981]). The ways to discover the historical project are to look in the narrative for: (1) the strategy of the movement, (2) the organizational principles for the group of followers, and (3) the enemies of the movement.

Before looking at these three points, let us state our hypothesis in brief fashion: The Jesus movement saw the principal obstacle to the realization of God's kingdom in Palestine to be the temple and the class structure that it supported. In the terms of our analysis, their focus was on the Asiatic social organization rather than on the contradiction between the Palestinian (Asiatic) society and the Roman (slave) one. The latter became for the movement a secondary contradiction. Because the class domination of the priests rested principally on a deep-seated ideology, the strategy of the Jesus movement was one of ideological attack. Our Gospels give ample evidence that Jesus was executed by a broad coalition of groups that for different reasons were threatened by this historical project. This is our hypothesis.

As we look at the Gospels to flesh out this hypothesis a bit we must remember that the fact that the Jesus group preached the coming of God's kingdom hardly distinguished them from several other groups in first-century Palestine. This was a time of turmoil, and the prophetic preaching of a kingdom of justice and peace fired Jewish imagination. Essenes, Pharisees, and Zealots all expected the imminent dawning of the kingdom. Only the Sadducees with their concern for the temple ritual were cool to these expectations. Though there were differences of emphasis as to the content of the coming kingdom, the main differences were in the analysis of the Palestinian social structure and the consequent adoption of strategies of faith. Here Jesus and his followers had something different to offer Galilean peasants.

First, let us briefly look at Jesus' strategy. In keeping with well-established conclusions of New Testament scholarship, we favor the account of the Synoptic Gospels in looking for this strategy. Jesus moved about Galilee, drawing from that society a small band of followers who left their occupations to go about with him. The favorite example for the gospel writers is that of Simon and Andrew, who left their fishing to become "fishers of men" (Mark 1:16–20). Jesus and his band were in constant movement, and their whereabouts were often not known to outsiders. For this movement they relied on the small fishing boats of some of the followers, in order to get away from the multitudes that pursued them seeking Jesus' reputed healing powers (Mark 4:35; 3:7, 13).

It is evident that the multitudes were important in their strategy both as the beneficiaries of the coming kingdom, as illustrated in his concern to feed and heal them, and as a recruiting ground for followers. But a distance was maintained by the constant movement of Jesus' band and by his teaching in parables: "To you has been given the secret of the kingdom of God, but for those outside everything is in parables" (Mark 4:11).

On the occasions in which the group went into one town or another they often ran into opposition from local representatives of the religious establishment, the "scribes and Pharisees" of the Gospels. Among many examples we can mention the healing of a paralytic at a house in Capernaum and the reaction it produced (Mark 2:1–12), and the incident over a man with a withered hand in a synagogue of an unnamed town (Mark 3:1–6).

Because of their analysis of the struggle as primarily one to be won on the ideological battleground, the movement needed the broadest possible contact with the people. This was surely the main reason for the constant movement they display. This also explains their occasional breaking up into teams of two to cover a larger territory (Mark 6:7–13; Luke 10:1–12). The preference for the hills, the wilderness, and the seashore are probably to be explained by the need for security, in case of pursuit, and also to avoid provoking local teachers of religion.

The second stage in the strategy of the Jesus movement is clearly marked in the Synoptic Gospels by the departure from Galilee in order to go to Jerusalem: "He went on his way through towns and villages, teaching, and journeying toward Jerusalem" (Luke 13:22); "on the way to Jerusalem he was passing along between Samaria and Galilee" (Luke 17:11); "and taking the twelve, he said to them, 'Behold, we are going up to Jerusalem, and everything that is written of the Son of man by the prophets will be accomplished' " (Luke 18:31); "as they heard these things, he proceeded to tell a parable, because he was near to Jerusalem, and because they supposed that the kingdom of God was to appear immediately" (Luke 19:11); "and when he had said this, he went on ahead, going to Jerusalem" (Luke 19:28); "and when he drew near and saw the city he wept over it" (Luke 19:41).

There is an intensity of purpose in the repetition of the direction of the group toward Jerusalem. Jerusalem, as we have seen, was the symbolic center of the "Asiatic" class system that prevailed in Palestine. The second stage in the movement's challenge to that system was to confront it at its most powerful point. The objective was not just the city but precisely the temple:

> And he entered the temple and began to drive out those who sold, saying, "It is written, 'My house shall be a house of prayer'; but you have made it a den of robbers" [Luke 19:45].

Several interpretations can be made of the attack on the temple business. Considering that the Roman soldiers could see all goings on in the temple from the Antonia fortress that overlooked it, it is unlikely that Jesus and his followers expected to take the temple. More likely, the intention was to dramatize their criticism of the temple before the multitude of pilgrims who were in the city for the festival of Passover. By attacking the banking and commercial aspects of the temple they were not attacking a minor sideshow. This was fundamental to the class system. It was by means of the trade and the taxes collected in the temple that the priests extracted the surplus labor of the peasants. Several of the teaching incidents put by the gospel writers in the context of the temple in that week have to do with money (Caesar's coin, the widow's mite, Judas Iscariot's bargain with the priests). The economic base of the temple's domination was challenged by Jesus and his movement.

In the gospel narrative, Jesus' movements during his stay in Jerusalem are very suggestive for understanding his strategy. During the day he went openly into the temple and sought contact with the multitudes that gathered there. This teaching was dramatized by the attack on the merchants. By this time, and as a result in part of his attack, Jesus' life was in danger: "And the chief priests and the scribes were seeking how to arrest him in stealth, and kill him, for they said, 'Not during the feast, lest there be a tumult of the people' " (Mark 14:1–2). Jesus was safe among the multitude, because he and his followers had achieved a measure of support. At night Jesus would withdraw, apparently to Bethany to the house of Simon the leper (Mark 14:3). This strategy of nightly withdrawal was broken when one of the members of the movement offered for a price to take his enemies to a place where he could be found away from the crowd.

According to the theological reading overlaid on the narrative, Jesus went to Jerusalem to die. For that reason it is not obvious in the Gospels that his strategy was precisely designed to avoid falling into the hands of his enemies. But the narrative is clear enough. The priests had no need of a traitor except to find the hiding places where Jesus went when the crowds had dispersed. This contradiction within the Gospels enables us to separate the narrative from what overlies it and uncover the strategy.

The strategy of the Jesus movement was interrupted during the second stage by Jesus' execution. What the intended third stage was can only be a matter of conjecture. It must have involved some means of consolidating the popular support they expected to gain by their confrontation with the temple personnel in Jerusalem. A further step, also untouched in the gospel narratives, would have faced the (for Jesus, secondary) contradiction with the Roman presence in Palestine. God's kingdom with its strong egalita-

Rome

rianism would have required dealing with this oppressive force sooner or later.

Meanwhile, during the phase of gathering support in Galilee and during the trip to Jerusalem, Jesus and his followers were embodying in their communal living the egalitarian principles of God's kingdom:

> You are not to be called rabbi, for you have one teacher, and you are all brethren. And call no man your father on earth, for you have one father who is in heaven. Neither be called masters, for you have one master, the Christ. He who is greatest among you shall be your servant, whoever exalts himself will be humbled, and whoever humbles himself will be exalted [Matt. 23:8-12].

Jesus

In the coming kingdom of God that Jesus was announcing, the poor would be exalted and the rich cast down (Luke 6:20-26). In the story of a rich man who asked to enter the kingdom, Jesus was quite harsh in insisting that he sell his goods, give them to the poor, and enter the movement as simply one of the brothers (Mark 10:17-22). In reflecting on his rejection, the text puts in Jesus' mouth that hard saying: "How hard it will be for those who have riches to enter the kingdom of God! . . . It is easier for a camel to go through the eye of a needle than for a rich man to enter the kingdom of God" (Mark 10:23-25).

Just as the demand for equality excluded the wealthy who were not ready to abandon their riches, it also excluded those who clung to the positions afforded them by their families. The need to break family ties to join the movement is dramatized by the story of Jesus' own distant attitude toward his mother (Mark 3:31-35). The same point is made

equality

in a more general manner in sayings (Mark 10:28–31; Luke 14:25–27) in which the willingness to abandon family position is made a condition for membership in the movement. The stress on equality within the movement is in keeping with our hypothesis that Jesus' affirmation of God's kingdom was a denial of the class structure that required privileges for the priests.

This brings us to an examination of the enemies of Jesus and his movement. Jesus' principal enemies were the Pharisees in Galilee and the priests in Jerusalem—in other words, the principal beneficiaries of the class system and the teachers of the religious ideology that supported it. Concerning the Pharisees the Gospels have many harsh words, though it is impossible to sort out what goes back to the Galilean days and what represents the anti-Jewish polemic of the church outside of Palestine:

> Woe to you, scribes and Pharisees, hypocrites! For you tithe mint and dill and cummin, and have neglected the weightier matters of the law, justice and mercy and faith [Matt. 23:23].
>
> Woe to you, scribes and Pharisees, hypocrites! For you are like whitewashed tombs, which outwardly appear beautiful, but within they are full of dead men's bones and all uncleanness. So you also outwardly appear righteous to men, but within you are full of hypocrisy and iniquity [Matt. 23:27–28].

The narrative also reflects many cases of confrontation with the Pharisees over Jesus' rather casual attitude toward the law. These are set in the period of the Galilean wanderings of Jesus' group.

The temple was the object of Jesus' attacks during his last week in Jerusalem. There is first of all the account of the attack on the banking operations of the temple. But there is preserved also a prophecy that the temple would be destroyed, and the accounts of the trial of Jesus record as one of the accusations that he announced the temple's destruction:

> And as he came out of the temple, one of his disciples said to him, "Look, Teacher, what wonderful stones and what wonderful buildings!" And Jesus said to him, "Do you see these great buildings? There will not be left here one stone upon another, that will not be thrown down" [Mark 13:1-2].

This hostility to the temple is a conspicuous theme of the Gospels, and fits with Jesus' analysis of the class situation of Palestine as that of domination by the priests.

Another of Jesus' enemies was the Roman authority, made personal in the procurator Pontius Pilate. The Gospels agree that Jesus was executed as a messianic claimant. This is quite understandable. During that century and the following there were many "messiahs" who were taken to fulfill Isaiah's promises that God would raise a descendant of David to sit on his throne. These were regularly the occasion for disturbances, and the Romans would have viewed any movement of this sort as a threat. The most important case was that of Simon Bar Cocheba, which set off a major rebellion A.D. 132. The title on Jesus' cross read, "the king of the Jews," a clear indication of why the Romans had him crucified. Mark informs us that during that Passover week there had been an armed uprising with some casualties (Mark 15:7). Besides Jesus, Pilate crucified two *lestai*, a word which can refer either to common highway robbers or to armed insurrectionists. In this case, in the wake of the Jerusalem uprising, probably the latter is correct. To the

Roman authorities Jesus appeared, like the Zealots, as a rebel.

The Gospels, however, make a clear distinction between Jesus and the Zealots. They report that the crowds at Jerusalem also saw a difference. Pilate is said to have offered them a choice between the Zealot Barabbas and Jesus, at which they chose the release of Barabbas. This was the same multitude for fear of which the priests did not capture Jesus in broad daylight. Of course, the multitude was manipulated by the priests and Pharisees. It is not hard to understand the desire of these two groups to do away with Jesus. Nor is it hard to understand the fears of the Roman authorities. But Jesus and his movement sought to speak for the masses who were oppressed both by the Romans and by the priests (with the assistance of the Pharisees). It is, then, a problem that the crowd should have allowed itself to be swayed by the enemies of Jesus.

The choice of the multitude between Jesus and Barabbas dramatizes the difference between two social analyses and two strategies of liberation, that of the Jesus movement and that of the Zealots. The crowd of the Gospels chose the Zealot option when forced to a choice between the two. It must remain an open question whether they were right, in terms of the historical possibilities of Jesus' strategy. But it is not difficult to understand their choice.

First of all, a large proportion of the population of Jerusalem depended on the temple for their livelihood.[41] This included a large crew of artisans and builders, for there was permanent building activity going on during this whole period. It included a large population that lived from servicing the pilgrims who came to the city (innkeepers, merchants in food and sacrificial animals, etc.). And it included the bankers and moneychangers who were the immediate object of Jesus' attack. This part of the multitude had a vested interest in the temple, and would reject Jesus' strategy in favor of one which aimed rather at the Romans.

Secondly, for many of even the poorest elements of the population, the Roman domination would have seemed more visible and opprobrious than that of the priests. This would have included many people among the pilgrims. Perhaps they sympathized with what the Jesus movement represented but, offered a choice, preferred the strategy of direct confrontation with Rome.

The result is well known. Led by the priests, the principal enemies of Jesus and his followers, the multitudes supported the charges of sedition before the Roman authorities, who executed Jesus. With the death of Jesus the movement entered into a new and difficult phase of re-evaluation that is mostly lost to us.

Before discussing the Zealot strategy for the kingdom of God, a word should be said about the principal alternative hypothesis about the nature of Jesus and his movement. This historical reading stresses the sayings of Jesus on making peace, finding his option to be that of reconciliation and nonviolence. Jesus advised his followers to learn to love their enemies (Matt 5:43–45). They were to seek forgiveness from those whom they had offended (Matt. 5:21–26). They were to suffer evil rather than retaliate (Matt. 5:38–42). According to the reading of the Gospels that makes this a way of nonviolence that Jesus taught as universally valid, Jesus did not intend to have enemies. Their enmity was due to their hostilities, and Jesus' only response was to avoid provocation.

This reading of the Gospels is attractive to a sector of the modern church. However, it does not seem to apply to what the gospel narrative tells us of Jesus. We would understand, rather, that here the Jesus movement was trying to distinguish its tactics from those of the Zealots. The Zealots saw the Roman presence as the principal cause of the oppression of the Palestinian population. And the only way to rid the country of a military domination was by military means. Jesus and his movement, however, did not see Rome as the principal enemy. In their priorities, it was first necessary to do away with the temple domination. For this, they had to avoid provoking military conflicts. Our hypothesis does not hold Jesus to have categorically rejected military tactics. It does hold that he did not espouse them for ridding the country of priestly oppression.

The other context for the sayings on forgiveness is that of the internal demands of the movement. This is clearly the context of the sayings on forgiveness and reconciliation in Matthew 18, including the injunction to forgive seventy times seven (Matt. 18:21–22). It seems that the demands of internal peace within the movement and the need to avoid provoking military intervention by the Romans can explain these texts that form the basis of the alternative hypothesis about Jesus.

Other Palestinian Strategies for the Kingdom of God. The destruction of the Jerusalem temple in the year 70 was the culmination of many of the events that had been taking place in Palestine during the early years of the Jesus movement. With this Roman victory over the holiest symbol of believers in Palestine, the messianic strategies of all Palestinian groups collapsed, with the partial exception of that of the Pharisees.

Jesus and his followers had tried to unite the people against the temple because they believed that *it* rather than the Romans was the primary source of Israel's oppression. For six centuries all the empires of the Near East had used the temple and its priests as instruments to dominate working people. In Jesus' view the temple was, as Jeremiah had put it at the beginnings of this system, a den of thieves and not the house of prayer for the nations, which was its original purpose (Jer. 7:11; Mark 11:17).

In one sense the destruction of the temple was a vindication of the Jesus movement. But only in a very minor sense. For its destruction to be part of the coming of God's kingdom, the working masses had to understand that the priests were their enemies and organize an alternative society. With Jesus' execution the real possibility of achieving this popular support for an alternative along the lines advanced by the Jesus movement disappeared. To survive, the Jesus movement soon abandoned the field and moved out of Palestine. Its strategy had failed well before the war broke out in A.D. 66.

The Sadducees followed a strategy of preserving within a Roman-dominated province a space for keeping up the liturgical life of the temple. They were the principal beneficiaries of the system and they owed their positions of hegemony to the imperial authorities. It was in their interest, then, to find ways of accommodating the Jewish tradition to the needs of the empire, widening as much as possible the temple's scope of action. Their political maneuvers responded to this strategy. They were always looking for alliances with those Roman leaders who were rising in the constant power struggles in Rome. As Roman impatience increased in the face of continual Jewish rebellion, the space for maneuvering was constantly narrowing. With the destruction of the temple, the Sadducee strategy was finished. History had proved their way to be a false one.

The Zealots also held the temple as the center of their vision of God's kingdom. Their strategy was, nevertheless, diametrically opposed to that of the Sadducees. They saw the physical presence of Roman troops in Palestine as a profanation of God's land and a blasphemous denial of Yahweh's sovereignty. So the first order of business for believers was the expulsion of the Roman presence. They were surely not unaware of Roman military superiority, but they were also convinced that God would struggle to restore his kingdom, as he had done in the days of Deborah and Gideon. With this conviction, they rushed into a truly suicidal struggle. They had their great opportunity in the year 66, when the Roman proconsul Gesius Florus withdrew from the temple treasury the sum of seventeen talents. This sacking, following as it did a long series of frictions between Jews and Romans, solidified the people behind the hard line the Zealots had been urging for sixty years. A considerable army was raised in Galilee to liberate that territory. Another force took the temple grounds and expelled the soldiers from the Antonia fortress that controlled the city. The high priest, who had appealed for moderation, was assassinated. There followed a series of victories that filled the people with euphoria. But, in the year 70, after long, hard battles, the Roman general Titus took the city and put an end to the brief existence of Jerusalem as a free city. This meant the failure also of the Zealot strategy.

The Essenes apparently joined in the broad coalition that faced the Romans in this war. They had long been waiting for the final war against the heathen. Their principal community near the Dead Sea was destroyed in the mopping-up operations by the Roman forces, and we hear no more from them.

Among the organized groups of Palestinian Judaism, only the Pharisees came through the war without a total collapse. Like the Zealots, Essenes, and Sadducees, they too believed in the temple. But the centers for their ongoing activities were the town synagogues. Here the faithful gathered every week to read the Scriptures, to hear interpretations of them, and to pray for their own redemption. Here the people learned how to live a pious life of obedience to the law of Moses. These village people would make the pilgrimage to Jerusalem to offer their sacrifices in the temple only on special occasions. The rest of the year they made the synagogue and its teaching the center of their religious life. This was also the territory where the Pharisees held the hegemony. When the temple was destroyed, the synagogues became the only centers of Jewish life. The Pharisees emerged from the ruins as the most prestigious group.

In order to rightly place the gospel polemic against the Pharisees, it is important to realize that they were the principal rivals of the church in the later period. Much of the bitterness expressed in the Gospels against the Pharisees must come from this context rather than from the original Jesus movement. This is not to deny that Jesus and his followers also attacked the Pharisees. These pious teachers of religion were not rich. They were not directly exploiting the Galilean people. But they were the transmitters in Galilee of the temple ideology that Jesus and his movement were attacking. For this reason the Jesus strategy collided with the Pharisees before it even became a factor for the priests in Jerusalem. This initial opposition between the Pharisees and the Jesus movement was deepened when Paul and other Christian missionaries began using the synagogues as recruiting grounds for the church in its missionary expansion. The synagogue survived the war as a viable institution and became the social base for rabbinic Judaism, which is the direct descendant of the Pharisaic movement.

About the Palestinian Jesus movement after Jesus' death our information is inadequate. Some things are known from the book of the Acts of the Apostles, and others can be deduced from the Gospels, especially the sayings common to Matthew and Luke. From Acts we know of the establishment in the urban context of Jerusalem of a community that institutionalized the egalitarian practice of the itinerant group that followed Jesus. They practiced a communism of consumption, sharing the goods that they had acquired by private means (Acts 2:44–45; 4:34–35). Their leaders were James, the brother of Jesus, and Peter, one of the twelve chosen by Jesus as his closest circle. They lived in the expectation of the return of the Lord in glory (Acts 3:17–21; 1:9–11). The Gospel of Mark bears witness to the belief that this return would take place in Galilee (Mark 14:28; 16:7). At that time the Lord would restore the kingdom to Israel (Acts 1:6). Surprisingly, the Jerusalem Jesus community maintained a life of prayer in and around the temple (Acts 2:46; 3:1; 21:17–26), although they were regarded with suspicion if not hostility by other worshipers there.

One sector within this community maintained the original hostility to the temple. Not surprisingly, it was against this sector that the earliest persecution of "Christians" by the priestly class was directed. Acts, chapters 6 and 7, tells of how Stephen was selected as a target by the priests (6:8–7:1), how he defended himself by appealing to the biblical tradition of attacks on the temple (7:2–53), and how he was eventually killed by stoning (7:54–60). The Jerusalem community of Christians seems to have been destroyed during the war—that is, whatever remained after the persecutions had led many to flee for their safety. At any rate, they do not appear to have played a significant role in the historic events that led up to the war.

Recently, Gerd Theissen has made a good case for the existence of a continued Jesus movement in Galilee.[42] Its leaders were itinerant radicals of the sort who had followed Jesus, and there were sympathizers who assisted them in the villages. But they had no historical importance either.

Much remains to be learned about the Palestinian sequel to Jesus and his movement. It seems likely that the current interest in a sociological approach to the works of antiquity and in an archaeology of the material base of daily life will increase our knowledge in the next generation. What we have said here is no more than suggestive. Our New Testament shows very little interest in the Palestinian Jesus movement, and directs our attention instead to the founding of the church outside of Palestine. This is the judgment of posterity on a movement we should like to know better. This judgment is historically correct at least insofar as it is a fact that the Jewish-Roman war wiped out any possibility of success the movement may have had in becoming the bearer of good news for the peasantry of Galilee. Although it is impossible to overturn such a decisive historical judgment, our interest remains because the Latin American popular movement of our day knows that it must learn even from historical failures if it is one day to succeed in establishing a just society.

6

The Internationalization of God's Kingdom

We have seen that the Palestinian Jesus movement lost all historical importance in the generation between Jesus' death and the Jewish-Roman war. But the story of Jesus and of his preaching of the coming of God's kingdom did not die out. It just shifted its sociological base. From being a movement of Galilean peasants that promised "good news" of a historical resolution to the long-standing Palestinian problem it became a very broad movement to resolve the spiritual problems of the mixed population of the cities of the Roman Empire. From being a rural movement it became an urban one. From being Aramaic-speaking it became Greek-speaking. From addressing itself to the historical problem of a coherent people, the Galilean peasantry burdened with class domination by priests and Romans, it now addressed itself to the spiritual problems of a very heterogeneous assortment of peoples with problems of insecurity, meaninglessness, and a lack of historical projects.

The expansion of what was to be known as Christianity throughout the cities of the empire was remarkable. It is also well known. What has been less clear to the general public is the dramatic transformation that this change in sociological base meant. One can hardly doubt that the urban masses of the empire had very serious problems. Many of them had been uprooted from their homelands by a conquering army in search of slave labor and thrown into an alien environment with peoples whose languages they did not know. Others had been one-time free peasants displaced from their lands by the growth of large privately-owned farms worked by imported slaves. And still others were small artisans and merchants who traveled in their pursuit of a livelihood. Such a heterogeneous group had no possibility of implementing any single historical project. It had no coherent structure and no common aim. Its common problem was a spiritual one, rootlessness and the uncertainties that accompanied it. The gospel of God as preached by the Galilean Messiah Jesus meant something quite different in this context than it had meant to the original Palestinian Jesus movement.

The Palestinian Jesus movement lived in the hope that Jesus their Messiah would return soon to Galilee to establish God's kingdom. It was a movement of the oppressed classes of Palestine, which focused their hope for their historical liberation. As such, the destruction of the independence movement during the war against Rome also meant the end of their project. For those who listened to the story of Jesus outside of Palestine, the destruction of the temple and the independence movement in Palestine meant instead the removal of the Jews from importance and the internationalization of the gospel. The gospel of God could no longer be taken as a Jewish messianic hope, but now appeared in a more spiritual form as a heavenly hope. In this form the gospel was a private hope that offered salvation for the soul, that most private of all spiritual entities. It no longer mattered whether or not the believers were Jews.

They were unique persons. The kingdom of God was built on this collection of individuals, where nationality became irrelevant. Jesus' attacks on the temple from this perspective seemed like attacks on the proud particularity of the Jews, who thought God's kingdom was for them. Once one ceased to think of the kingdom as a historical project, such an insistence looked like the most irrational sort of national pride. Thus the destruction of the temple now looked like God's judgment on the inexplicable pride of the Jewish people.

We must briefly outline the manner in which the new social base of the gospel account, now carried by a heterogeneous urban population, led to a spiritualizing of God's kingdom. We shall attempt to do this quickly by looking at three New Testament theologians, Paul, the author of the Epistle to the Hebrews, and John. They represent three ways of articulating the gospel of the spiritual kingdom in which the new international movement believed.

Paul. Besides being its most important agent, the industrious missionary Paul is our principal witness to the transformation of the good news. For Paul and the churches he founded in cities like Corinth and Ephesus, the center of the gospel was paradoxically the cross of the Christ (1 Cor. 1:17-31). For the Palestinian Jesus movement the crucifixion of the Messiah had been a problem that had stopped the momentum they were gaining. For Paul it was no such thing, but the very center of God's plan for humankind: "For I decided to know nothing among you except Jesus Christ and him crucified" (1 Cor. 2:2); "I have been crucified with Christ; it is no longer I who live, but Christ who lives in me" (Gal. 2:20).

This proved to be a powerful message for the aimless and suffering urban masses. God himself had entered through his Christ into their sufferings! According to Paul's preaching, the real suffering that these people knew was but a reflection of the universal human condition. From the time of the first man Adam, sin had ruled over humanity collectively and over each individual in particular: "Therefore as sin came into the world through one man and death through sin, so death spread to all men because all have sinned" (Rom. 5:12). Death is the final expression of sin. As death is a universal fate of humankind, so salvation must offer a solution that is universally applicable. To save humanity from its spiritual captivity God sent his Christ (the Greek form of the word "messiah," but with a new content) to die in expiation for the sins of humanity. So the cross in this preaching is the aim of Jesus' whole activity, and its centrality corresponds to the misery ("death") that is so characteristic of those masses to whom Paul preaches.

The person to whom Paul addresses his message is no longer "the poor" but rather "the sinner." And because sin is a universal human condition since the sin of Adam, the gospel is actually addressed without distinction to all humankind, to every person. All have sinned and are liable to the judgment of God. For that reason Christ died in order to free humankind from the anger that God will direct at his chosen moment against sin:

> While we were yet helpless, at the right time Christ died for the ungodly. Why, one will hardly die for a righteous man—though perhaps for a good man one will dare even to die. But God shows his love for us in that while we were yet sinners Christ died for us. Since, therefore, we are now justified by his blood, much more shall we be saved by him from the wrath of God [Rom. 5:6–9].

Each person has sinned individually. Christ died for this totality of human individuals. In order to achieve salvation, each individual believer must identify with the cross of Christ in the hope of sharing with Christ in his resurrection:

> Do you not know that all of us who have been baptized into Christ Jesus were baptized into his death? We were buried therefore with him by baptism into death, so that as Christ was raised from the dead by the glory of the Father, we too might walk in newness of life. For if we have been united with him in a death like his, we shall certainly be united with him in a resurrection like his [Rom. 6:3–5].

It is natural that in so individually-centered a message the very term "kingdom," which was so central to the Jesus movement, should tend to disappear.

It was also natural that in a salvation addressed to individuals, the historical differences among groups should lose importance: "Here there cannot be Greek and Jew, circumcised and uncircumcised, barbarian, Scythian, slave, free man, but Christ is all, and in all" (Col. 3:11). Each individual before God is separated from his national and class group and made to appear in his separateness. This looks very much like a religious expression of the social reality of the urban population of the empire. Among that population were slaves torn from their native social contexts in Africa, Asia, and Europe. Present also were the large number of unemployed peasants who had lost their lands in the transition from village to slave labor. This large group of free men depended on the "bread and circuses" welfare policy of the government for its survival, and had no contribution to make to society except by joining the armed forces and thereby also leaving their native lands.

An important segment of the Christian churches was that of merchants and artisans, who were economically independent and could offer their houses as meeting places for the Christian groups.[43] Like the middle classes in most societies, these people had no historical project of their own. Their occupations often took them away from their natural social settings, as was notably the case with the scattered Jewish people. For these various sectors that made up Paul's churches, a message that subordinated national differences and heightened the individual's responsibility for his or her own salvation made a lot of sense.

The subordination of differences in the Christian community did not extend to the real social relations in the public world. Paul in his letter to Philemon is concerned about returning to his brother in Christ the slave Onesimus, who had run away. Onesimus is to be received and treated as a spiritual brother, but he need not be granted his formal liberty. In spite of Paul's insistence that all Christians are brothers and sisters, he does not require the freeing of slaves: "Masters, treat your slaves justly and fairly, knowing that you also have a master in heaven" (Col. 4:1); "Were you a slave when called? Never mind. But if you can gain your freedom, avail yourself of the opportunity" (1 Cor. 7:21). What counted before God was the inner person transformed by union with Christ—not external relations. The kingdom of God, already present in anticipation in these Christian communities, came to be a transformed spiritual reality withdrawn from the concrete relations of production.

In this new incarnation, the gospel of Jesus Christ became a religious faith in competition with the Greek philosophies, the mystery religions, and Judaism itself for the support of the same unclassed and neglected masses. Each "philosophy" offered an individual salvation that it declared to be truer and better than the others. It was in this context that Paul entered into a rivalry with Judaism that is reflected in most of his Epistles. But at the same time that Paul was competing in this pluralistic world with the Jews of the dispersion he had also a rear-guard struggle with the Jesus movement that still survived in Palestine and that was waiting for Christ's return to restore the kingdom to Israel. The rigors of this struggle are recorded in Acts 15 and 21–26, and especially in Paul's Epistle to the Galatians. For Paul and his followers Jesus' attack on the temple was understood as an attack on the particularism of Judaism as a religion. Jesus' disputes with the Pharisees in Galilee were understood as the beginning of the religious competition between a rabbinical Judaism of obedience to the law, and a new religion of salvation through identification with the sacrifice of the Christ on the cross. The new milieu gave a new meaning to the gospel story.

An example of this is Paul's stress on virtuous living as the demonstration of those who are to enter the kingdom. In the gospel story, the kingdom of God was promised to the poor, a fact well illustrated by Jesus' parable of the poor Lazarus who was received in Abraham's bosom while the rich man whose crumbs he ate was not (Luke 16:19–31). No mention is made in the parable of the virtue or lack thereof on the part of Lazarus. He was poor, and that qualified him for the kingdom. For entry into a spiritual kingdom, individual right living is of the essence:

> Do you not know that the unrighteous will not inherit the kingdom of God? Do not be deceived; neither the immoral, nor idolators, nor adulterers, nor homosexuals, nor thieves, nor the greedy, nor drunkards, nor revilers, nor robbers will inherit the kingdom of God [1 Cor. 6:9–10].

Now the works of the flesh are plain: immorality, impurity, licentiousness, idolatry, sorcery, enmity, strife, jealousy, anger, selfishness, dissension, party spirit, envy, drunkenness, carousing and the like. I warn you, as I warned you before, that those who do such things shall not inherit the kingdom of God [Gal. 5:19–21].

Although Paul's doctrine of the human person is a complex one, much more so than the simple Platonic opposition of soul and body, it remains clear that he thinks of individuals as entering the kingdom of God on their own and not as part of organized groups. This is one meaning of his stress on its spiritual character: "I tell you this, brethren: flesh and blood cannot inherit the kingdom of God, nor does the perishable inherit the imperishable" (1 Cor. 15:50). From this it is clear that he does not think of God's kingdom as a historical project, but as the end of history, to be entered by purified persons.

A final example of the transformation undergone by the gospel preached by the Jesus movement when it left its Palestinian context is the resurrection. According to most studies of the subject, belief in individual resurrection entered Jewish belief at the time of the Maccabean uprising. Those who were giving their lives in a bloody struggle against heathen tyranny were assured that they would share in the kingdom they were founding. A dramatic testimony to this faith is the story in 2 Maccabees 7 of the martyrdom of seven brothers before the eyes of their mother. As both Judaism and the gospel of Jesus moved into the urban setting of the non-Palestinian ancient world, the resurrection became a "biblical" version of the immortality taught by the philosophers. In Platonism and its popular versions immortality of the soul was a way of affirming the primacy of the individual human person with a unique individuality.

When the fleshly shell of the body was destroyed by death, the pure person would survive in a better form. History with its change and its passions could not touch the soul if it was disciplined by philosophy.

In the context of dispersion-Judaism and Hellenistic Christianity the belief in the resurrection was cut off from its original political context and made a similar affirmation of the value of the individual person. The resurrection itself, rather than God's kingdom, often became the content of salvation. One did not so much believe in the resurrection as an assurance of participation in the coming kingdom as believe in the resurrection as the assurance of the permanence of one's true self.

In the competition of religions of individual salvation, Christianity had an advantage over Judaism. Once it broke away from its Jewish origins, it appealed to the masses as a spiritual religion not burdened by the national feelings of the Jewish people. The destruction of the Jesus community in Jerusalem and the Jesus movement in Galilee during the war left a Christian church totally severed from Palestinian politics and ready to claim the masses of the broad urban world. The writings of the New Testament all reflect to a greater or lesser extent this new context. Even the Synoptic Gospels, which preserve and rework traditional materials which came out of Palestine, show an overlay of spiritualistic and unhistorical religion. In this overlay of the older narrative, Jesus becomes a Messiah who had to die by a divine design pre-announced by the prophets (Mark 8:31; 10:45; Luke 24:25–26, etc.).

The Epistle to the Hebrews. This little treatise offers a variant on the spiritual gospel that the church preached to the urban masses. Basic to its theology is the conviction that what is true is immaterial, that which cannot be touched. The palpable is merely an imitation of the immaterial original. This is a popularization and Christianization of a view widely diffused in antiquity by Platonists of various sorts.

Much rests on an idea briefly presented in the Sinai texts of the book of Exodus, that Moses was shown the original temple on the mountain after which he was to pattern the tabernacle and its implements (Exod. 25:40). The attacks of the gospel narrative against the temple are understood as a criticism of the faith of those who place their confidence in the copy instead of looking to the heavenly original: "They serve a copy and shadow of the heavenly sanctuary" (Heb. 8:5). On the contrary, Jesus is understood to have entered the heavenly original, and there to have offered a perfect sacrifice for the expiation of all human sins. The idea seems to be that the crucifixion was but an earthly reflection of this eternal sacrifice:

> But when Christ appeared as a high priest of the good things that have come, then through the greater and more perfect tent (not made with hands, that is, not of this creation) he entered once for all into the Holy Place, taking not the blood of goats and calves but his own blood, thus securing an eternal redemption. For if the sprinkling of defiled persons with the blood of goats and bulls and with the ashes of a heifer sanctifies for the purification of the flesh, how much more shall the blood of Christ, who through the eternal Spirit offered himself without blemish to God, purify your conscience from dead works to serve the living God [Heb. 9:11–14].

God's kingdom is understood here as a heavenly reality, and as such, unshakeable: "Therefore let us be grateful for receiving a kingdom that cannot be shaken" (Heb. 12:28).

As unshakeable it contrasts with the holy mount Sinai, which trembled at the approach of God (Heb. 12:18–21). God's kingdom is an immaterial and celestial reality.[44]

John. The third theologian of this New Testament Christianity is the evangelist John. The interpretation of the fourth Gospel continues to be uncertain because of the failure so far of the attempts to locate it sociologically.[45] Nevertheless, the tendency toward making salvation not only individual but also a matter of right belief is unmistakable. It was this tendency that became radicalized in the important movement identified as Gnosticism by the second-century church fathers.

The term "kingdom of God" almost disappears in this version of the gospel, to be replaced by that of "eternal life." Long recognized by a certain stream of Christianity as a summary of this gospel is John 3:16:

> For God so loved the world that he gave his only Son, that whoever believes in him should not perish but have eternal life.

For our purposes, the important points about this statement are the terms for the hoped-for salvation (eternal life) and the means to achieve it (believing in Jesus the Christ or Son of God). The full scope of eternal life as understood by this gospel is far beyond our possibility of quick explanation. However, it is an individual goal, as is salvation for Paul. The stress on right belief is much greater than for Paul, but is again an individualizing tendency. Jesus is the Word incarnate, and only those who believe this have eternal life. Those who deny that Jesus Christ truly came in the flesh are not of God (1 John 4:1–3). True believers both confess that he came in the flesh and recognize that he existed before the creation and is the only-begotten Son of God (John 1:1–14).

John's famous style reflects his theology. Jesus regularly talks with persons who fail to understand him: Nicodemus does not see how he can enter the womb of his mother and be reborn. The Samaritan woman does not see how Jesus can draw life-giving water with no pail, etc. The mystery of belief is that only those who are born of the spirit, or born from above, can believe. The tendency (not fully realized) is to reduce salvation to the possession of a small circle of true believers.

(elitism)

"Kingdom of God" is a purely residual term in this Gospel. It survives (three times, all in John 3) only because of its centrality in the earlier gospel narrative. But its meaning is quite transformed:

> Truly, truly, I say to you, unless one is born from above [or, born anew], he cannot see the kingdom of God [John 3:3].

To Pilate Jesus affirms that his kingdom is not of this world (John 18:36). To think that his could be a historical kingdom is an error of persons who are blind to spiritual truths because they have not been born of the Spirit (John 3:3–12).

(spiritual kingdom)

This is a powerful religious message but it is certainly disconnected from any historical project, that of the Galilean peasantry or any other. John is just as far as Paul or the author of Hebrews from the original Jesus movement, whatever may be the geographical and sociological base of this Gospel.

Let us summarize this chapter: It has been our hypothesis that the Jesus movement was one of several responses to the oppression that the peasants of Palestine bore in the first century of the Christian Era. With the execution of Jesus, the momentum of the movement was lost, and the movement itself was wiped out as a historical factor by the war of 66–70. Nevertheless, through the efforts of people attracted

(summary)

by the gospel account who were not tied to the Galilean peasantry, the story of Jesus and his preaching of God's kingdom was widely spread through the cities of the empire. In the process the "good news" of the kingdom became a spiritual message of individual salvation. In this unhistorical form it has been justly characterized as a religious opium, because it enables a suffering people to endure, by offering private dreams to compensate for an intolerable public reality.

7

What Is to Be Done?

In abstract and general terms, God's kingdom means in the Bible a society of justice, equality, and abundance. In concrete terms, it directs different historical projects under different circumstances. At two seminal moments the kingdom meant liberation, a struggle against class systems that systematically exploited the working people of Israel.

First of all, in Canaan, to accept Yahweh as the king of Israel meant to repudiate the kings who were exploiting the productive villages and along with the kings to reject the religious superstructure that gave them legitimacy. For the rebellious peasants of Israel, God had revealed himself in Egypt as a liberator, and they found it impossible to worship Yahweh and also accept the kings who were exploiting and enslaving them. Inspired by this Yahweh, Canaanite peasants rose up and formed tribal alliances to face their exploiters. However, this project was subverted from within when David of Judah, in the name of Yahweh, founded a dynasty stronger and more powerful than those rejected by the tribes of Israel. In this new order, Yahweh's kingdom became the ideological support for the exploitation of working people.

In the first century of the Christian Era, under the impact of Roman oppression, God's kingdom once again became the inspiration for rebellion and the promise of liberation. Still, none of the strategies to make the kingdom a reality was successful. Jesus and his movement did not achieve the mass support needed to set in motion their historical project before it was cut off by Jesus' crucifixion. The Zealots had their moment of glory when they consolidated the rebel forces in an armed struggle, but they were defeated by the superior military power of Rome. And the Pharisees and their rabbinical successors have continued to wait for the kingdom for centuries. From the messianic Jesus movement there arose a universal, spiritual, and individualistic religion that offers inner salvation to oppressed men and women within various class systems.

These are the materials concerning God's kingdom with which we have to work. What real possibilities do they offer the poor in our day?

In the first place, this biblical investigation has placed tools in our hands for the necessary task of unmasking religion that conceals and justifies domination. We have learned how Yahweh's kingdom could be used as an ideological support for an oppressive regime in Israel. We have learned how, in the analysis made by the Jesus movement, the temple of Yahweh and its religion had become the principal enemies of the liberating kingdom of Yahweh. Then we saw how this rebellious message was deflected toward a religion that was individualistic, spiritualizing, and ahistorical. It was in this form that it was presented to the urban, uprooted working people of the empire. And this was done in the name of Jesus the Messiah and of the kingdom he proclaimed.

All of this should put us on guard against a preaching of a

gospel that may not be good news. We will not find protection against this problem in biblical language or right doctrine. Even within the Bible, God's kingdom was exploited for quite different purposes. It is necessary to look critically at what is being proclaimed in our day as good news for the poor. We should learn to ask, "What are its real consequences in history?" The answer to this question can hardly be given in general terms. It must be formulated by each Christian group in its place, in the light of its historical juncture.

Even so, the general statement can safely be made that Protestant churches in Latin America have been the allies of imperialism. In order to penetrate traditional societies, monopoly capital has needed to break the bonds of solidarity and to create individuals who lead their lives as personal projects. For this it has found Protestantism useful, and we have often not seen how we were being used. Comparable judgments could be made of Catholic Christianity. Therefore, an important continuation of this study of the kingdom of God in the Bible will be the analysis within each group of the shape that the kingdom takes in *its* preaching and *its* practice.

In the second place, our biblical investigation shows the need for conjunctural analysis and the formulation of strategies of liberation based on it. Such strategies cannot be formulated in abstraction from an understanding of the mechanisms of oppression. Jesus and the Zealots formulated different strategies of liberation because they understood the conjuncture of first-century Palestine differently. We cannot know whether Jesus' strategy had more possibility of success than that of the Zealots. That is not what is important. Neither the one nor the other can be applied to our dependent capitalism. We must make an analysis of our

situation in order to formulate relevant strategies of liberation. In doing so, we can count on a significant liberating
tradition within our sacred texts. But the Bible will do
neither our analyzing nor our strategizing. This is the task
of Christian groups in their particular places.

The first task, that of unmasking the ideological uses of
the "gospel," is a necessary preparation for the second
task. These tasks must be carried out together with people
committed to liberation who are not necessarily believers.
In its original biblical expression, God's kingdom was for
the poor and not for believers.

We take for granted that analysis and strategy will be part
of a political practice of struggle for liberation. There remains a third task peculiar to the community of faith. This
is the task of theological production. We need to articulate
theoretically the nature and work of the God who freed
Israel from the Egyptian Pharaoh and from the Canaanite
kings. This involves criticism of a theology done for a
dominating church. Over against the self-sufficient creator
God of a church that felt itself mistress of society and at
peace with the natural world, we must affirm a God who is
historical and who actively strives to arouse the oppressed
and to destroy their oppressors. Classical philosophy and
theology must be examined for its class content. This is a
somewhat technical task for which we shall need persons
well equipped biblically and philosophically. But, to be
valid, the task must be carried out in close contact with
working people who are struggling for their liberation.

Only experience will tell if the biblical kingdom of God
can be truly good news for the poor, the exploited workers
of Latin America. There seem to be some positive elements
here, but only their incarnation in effective strategies of liberation will confirm that this is not a matter of illusions, of
stones when the people ask for bread. The liberation of the

people of Latin America is imposed on us today, and for those who believe in God's kingdom we have a divine ally in our struggle. History must say whether our faith is well placed. "The proof of the pudding is in the eating."

Notes

1. The tradition of the Fathers of the Church and the majority opinion among modern interpreters is that Mark wrote his Gospel in Rome. Ireneaus, bishop of Lyons, informs us (*Adv. haer.* III, 1.2) that this happened after the death of Peter (A.D. 64), and in this the chaotic situation of Jerusalem described in Mark 13 offers confirmation. Most commentators think that the Gospel was written during the war (66–70) but before its final outcome. Some, among them Wellhausen, Brandon, and Belo, consider that Mark 13 already presupposes a knowledge of the destruction of the temple and that therefore the correct date of composition is a little after 70. With Werner Georg Kummel we can conclude cautiously: "Since there are no decisive arguments for a year before or after 70, we must be content to conclude that Mark was written around 70" (*Introduction to the New Testament,* Nashville: Abingdon, 1966, p. 71).

2. We are in possession of multiple copies of this myth, the Enuma Elish. It is edited and translated into English in *Ancient Near Eastern Texts Relating to the Old Testament,* ed. James B. Pritchard (Princeton: Princeton University Press, 1950), pp. 60–72. Some clay tablets with ritual instructions for the festival have also survived. See ibid., pp. 331–34.

3. We quote from the Revised Standard Version of the Bible in this and other quotations in this book, unless otherwise indicated.

4. The rabbinical references are brought together and commented by Norman H. Snaith, *The Jewish New Year Festival* (London, 1948).

5. Commentators have often supposed that the Psalms were the private prayers of David and other pious men of ancient times. Nineteenth-century liberal biblical criticism tended to see here the "hasidim," sectarian groups within post-exilic Juda-

ism. In the twentieth century the great Norwegian scholar Sigmund Mowinckel in his *Psalmenstudien* (Oslo, 1921–24) has led the way to seeing that for the most part we have to do with genuine hymns and prayers from communal worship, and that at the Jerusalem temple in pre-exilic monarchical times. The date of at least some psalms, the royal ones (Psalms 2, 18, 20, 21, 45, 72, 89, 110), can be none other because of the major role of the king in them.

6. Here, as elsewhere in our quotations, we correct RSV's "Lord" to the äpproximate Hebrew form of God's name in Israel, "Yahweh."

7. The liturgical significance of the group of "enthronement psalms" was first seen by Mowinckel, in the second of his *Psalmenstudien*. Some biblical scholars are still not convinced of the practice of Yahweh's annual enthronement. The dispute hinges on the relationship of these psalms to the similar motif in the writings of the Second Isaiah (Isaiah 40–55). Mowinckel understood that the prophet was inspired for his oracles by the liturgical celebration of Yahweh's kingship. This seems a most natural conclusion. Georg Fohrer and others think that the influence goes in the opposite direction, and that the enthronement psalms are post-exilic celebrations of an eschatological, future coming of Yahweh the eternal king.

8. RSV translates the Hebrew perfect as a present verb. This is due to a nonliturgical interpretation of the psalm, and we have corrected it.

9. A good comparative study has been made by Werner Schmidt, "Königtum Gottes in Ugarit und Israel," *Beihefte zur Zeitschrift für die Alttestamentliche Wissenschaft* (Berlin, 1961); hereafter referred to as BZAW.

10. We are following the typology of the great modern historian of religion Mircea Eliade, in his *Patterns in Comparative Religion* (New York: Sheed & Ward, 1958), ch. 2, pp. 38–123.

11. The way in which justice in the ancient Near Eastern culture was a characteristic of creation, as the righting of chaos, is amply documented by Hans Heinrich Schmidt, *Gerechtigkeit als Weltordnung* (Tübingen: Mohr, 1968).

12. For the whole subject, see F. Charles Fensham, "Widow, Orphan, and the Poor in Ancient Near Eastern Legal and Wis-

dom Literature," *Journal of Near Eastern Studies* 21 (1962): 129–139.

13. On the subject of this cult, see Martin Buber, *Kingship of God,* trans. Richard Scheimann (New York: Harper, 1973), pp. 94–98, 177–84 (German original of 1932).

14. Jer. 7:31; 19:4–5; 32:35; Lev. 20:1–5. The cult is in both places referred to by the name *molek,* a distortion of *melek* (king) with the vowels of *bošet* (shame). A similar phenomenon is the distortion of the name of Išbaal son of Saul (1 Chron. 9:39) into Išbošet (2 Sam. 2:8), "man of Baal" into "man of shame."

15. The book of Jeremiah regards the king of this cult to have been, not Yahweh, but Baal. Nevertheless, Ezek. 20:25–26 shows that for those engaged in this rite the sacrifice was considered to be done in obedience to Yahweh. The editors of the book of Jeremiah did not think it possible that such a cult could have been addressed to Yahweh.

16. A cult that was known to Israel and that had some influence in the Jerusalem court was the Ammonite cult to their King-God. The Hebrew text of the Bible knows this god as Milkom (1 Kings 11:5, 33; 2 Kings 23:13). He was worshipped in Jerusalem. Apparently, the editors understood the expression *malkam* ("their king") as a proper noun, and to make it so vocalized the text as *milkom.* For this cult, cf. G. C. O'Ceallaigh, "And So David Did to All the Cities of Ammon," *Vetus Testamentum* 12 (1962): 179–89.

17. Norman K. Gottwald, *The Tribes of Yahweh: A Sociology of the Religion of Liberated Israel, 1250–1050 B.C.E.* (Maryknoll, N.Y.: Orbis, 1979). This work has confirmed and given with its impressive scholarship new solidity to the general position assumed in this book. The English version has been revised to take into account some of Gottwald's contributions.

18. Martin Buber first pointed out the decisive importance of this brief text in his *Kingship of God.*

19. Here we follow a conjectural textual emendation. The Hebrew text has Cushan-Rishataim as king of Aram, which seems unlikely. The difference in Hebrew script between Aram and Edom is minimal.

20. In its present form, 1 Samuel 8–12 shows signs of

Deuteronomistic editing (sixth century B.C.). This does not alter its value as a testimony to the preservation of the libertarian and antimonarchical tradition of Israel's origins. See Dennis J. McCarthy, "The Inauguration of Monarchy in Israel: A Form-Critical Study of 1 Samuel 8–12," *Interpretation* 27 (1973): 401–12.

21. Though covenant has long been the subject of theological scholarship, recent treatments derive largely from the seminal essay by George E. Mendenhall, *Law and Covenant in the Ancient Near East* (1955), reprinted in the *Biblical Archaeologist Reader 3* (New York: Doubleday, 1970), pp. 3–53. The literature on Israelite covenants and the treaties among Near Eastern kings is tremendous. In Spanish a summary statement is José Severino Croatto's *Alianza y experiencia salvífica* (Buenos Aires: Paulinas, 1964). A handy review of scholarly viewpoints is Dennis J. McCarthy's *Old Testament Covenant: A Survey of Current Opinions* (Oxford: Blackwell, 1972).

22. Exodus 34 has the Yahwist version of the ten commandments. The Yahwist strand of the Pentateuch took form in the tenth century. The more familiar form of the ten commandments in Exodus 20 is probably Elohist, which reached final form in the ninth or eighth century. The prohibition against the worship of other gods heads the list of commandments both in the Yahwist and in the Elohist version (and in its parallel in Deut. 5).

23. Much has been written on the *'apiru* question. Recent and important works are George E. Mendenhall, *The Tenth Generation: The Origins of the Biblical Traditions* (Baltimore: Johns Hopkins, 1973), pp. 122–41, and Gottwald *The Tribes of Yahweh,* pp. 401–9.

24. To Albrecht Alt we owe some truly pathfinding studies of the implications of the study of population distribution on the origins of Israel. The most important pieces are "Die Landnahme der Israeliten in Palästina" and "Erwägungen über die Landnahme der Israeliten in Palästina," both in his *Kleine Schriften zur Geschichte des Volkes Israel* (Munich, 1959), I, pp. 89–125 and 126–75, respectively. These studies first appeared in 1925 and 1939.

25. For this mode of production, see Roger Bartra, ed., *El modo de producción asiático: Antología de textos sobre proble-*

mas de la historia de los países coloniales (Mexico: Era, 1969). The concept comes from Marx, and its name from the fact that Marx encountered it in India.

26. Recent research on Israel's social organization and on the covenant renewal festival has been dominated by Martin Noth's productive theory that the Israelite tribal league should be understood on the model of Greek and pre-Roman amphictyonies. See Martin Noth, *Das System der zwolf Stämme Israels* (Stuttgart, 1930), and also his *History of Israel* (New York: Harper, 1958). Two fundamental elements of the analogy were the existence of a single central sanctuary (which in Israel's case could move around with the ark of the covenant) and the necessity of having twelve and always twelve members to the tribal league. The covenant at Shechem was interpreted as a ceremony that periodically renewed the mutual obligations among the twelve member tribes. However, the early texts (the stories in Judges) show neither that twelve was a fixed number nor that the ark played such a dominant role. And the ceremony in Joshua 24 does not mention mutual obligations among the tribes. What has been a very fruitful hypothesis is now being widely abandoned. For the reasons, see Georg Fohrer, "Altes Testament, 'Amphiktyonie' und 'Bund'?" in his *Studien zur Alttestamentlichen Theologie und Geschichte* (1949–1966) (BZAW, Berlin, 1969), and A.D.H. Mayes, *Israel in the Period of the Judges,* Studies in Biblical Theology (Naperville: Allenson, 1974).

27. This whole discussion of the Philistines has been greatly enriched by Gottwald, *Tribes,* pp. 410–25 and 655–58.

28. The best study of the significance of David's conquest of Jerusalem is that of Albrecht Alt, "Jerusalems Aufstieg," *Kleine Schriften,* III, 243–257.

29. For the administrative measures of David, see Gottwald, *Tribes,* pp. 362–67.

30. Cf. Gonzalo Puente Ojea, *Ideología e historia: La formación del cristianismo primitivo como fenómeno ideológico* (Madrid: Siglo XXI, 1974): "It is thus an essential part of every ideology to assume a utopian horizon in which it integrated and confirmed the sum total of its formulations, so that situations of dominance and dependency can be inserted, with a greater or lesser degree of likelihood, in an axiological context deceptively

acceptable for the classes negatively set apart as victims of the processes of alienation of consciousness, without which exploitation is not possible in the long run" (pp. 65–66).

31. Several modifications in the RSV translations of the verbs have been made to render consistently as petitions (optatives) the Hebrew imperfect tenses.

32. According to the inscription on the "Cyrus cylinder" found in Babylon and translated in Pritchard, *Ancient Near Eastern Texts*, pp. 315–16.

33. After two centuries of scholarly debate over these remarkable sayings it has now been established that they are the work of a great prophet of the Jewish exile community in Babylon during the sixth century B.C. There is ample proof of the stylistic and thematic coherence that unites these sayings and distinguishes them from the rest of the book of Isaiah.

34. See Otto Eissfeldt, "The Promises of Grace to David in Isaiah 55:1–5," in *Israel's Prophetic Heritage: Essays in Honor of James Muilenburg*, ed. B. W. Anderson and W. Harrelson (London: SCM Press, 1962), pp. 196–207.

35. An impressive analysis of these prophetic texts has recently been given us by Paul D. Hanson, *The Dawn of Apocalyptic: The Historical and Sociological Roots of Jewish Apocalyptic Eschatology* (Philadelphia: Fortress Press, 1975).

36. In speaking of the Jesus movement rather than of the person of Jesus himself, we are stressing the fact that it is the social fact, of which the person is to be sure a part, that has historical importance. It is a bourgeois admiration for heroic personalities that focused much of New Testament research on the person of Jesus. It is a virtue of the recent work of Gerd Theissen to have pointed again to the importance of the movement. See his *Sociology of Early Palestinian Christianity* (Philadelphia: Fortress Press, 1978; German original of 1977). His hypothesis about the nature of the Jesus movement is very different from ours, but the virtue of his work is that he asks the right questions. This is a major advance over most previous New Testament scholarship.

37. The "search for the historical Jesus" has occupied many a liberal scholar dissatisfied with the Christ preached in the Christian churches. In his famous 1906 book, *Von Reimarus zu Wrede*, Albert Schweitzer showed the very high proportion of the projec-

tion of our desires that was present in the investigations of the great scholars of the nineteenth century (See the English translation, *The Quest of the Historical Jesus* [London: A. and C. Black, 1910]. In spite of this unmasking, the search has not ended, and it is unlikely to end while there are liberal Christians in need of a great personality for inspiration.

38. In our study, we are going to rely especially on the work of the Portuguese scholar Fernando Belo, *Lecture matérialiste de l'évangile de Marc* (Paris: Cerf, 1974), available in Spanish from Editorial Verbo Divino of Estella, Navarra, in a 1975 edition and now also available in English from Orbis Books. An important aspect of Belo's method is his examination of the narrative of the Gospel as a form with a history, and his focus on that narrative, in distinction from a search for the person Jesus or for the words themselves of Jesus. Much form criticism has focused on isolated pericopes and taken the structure to be a product of the final redaction. Belo shows that the sayings lose their significance when taken out of the narrative. The narrative has suffered the fate of all transmitted material, but it has its integrity, which makes possible a tentative history of the narrative. It is this basic narrative that interests us.

39. A classic and still useful description of the slave mode of production is that of the German Marxist Karl Kautsky, *Foundations of Christianity*, trans. Henry F. Mins (New York: S. A. Russell, 1953; German original, 1910). Kautsky's understanding of Christianity has basic flaws, though it is still suggestive. The best portion of his work is his analysis of the productive base of the Roman Empire.

40. On the Zealots, see S. G. F. Brandon, *Jesus and the Zealots* (New York: Scribner's, 1967), and the works of Martin Hengel, especially *Die Zeloten* (Leiden: Brill, 1961).

41. For documentation on the place of the temple in the economic life of Jerusalem, see Joachim Jeremias, *Jerusalem in the Time of Jesus* (Philadelphia: Fortress Press, 1969; German original, 1923).

42. Theissen, *Sociology of Early Palestinian Christianity.*

43. The social composition of the Christian churches of the cities of the empire has just recently become the center of investigation by New Testament scholars. A good introduction and sum-

mary of the provisional conclusions of this research is Abraham J. Malherbe, *Social Aspects of Early Christianity* (Baton Rouge: Louisiana State University Press, 1977).

44. See James W. Thompson, " 'That Which Cannot Be Shaken': Some Metaphysical Assumptions in Hebrews 12:27," *Journal of Biblical Literature* 94 (1975): 580–587.

45. An important beginning is the analysis of the various groups that are represented by the persons in the Johannine gospel narrative: "the Jews," Nicodemus (secret believers), Jewish Christians, "the beloved disciple" (the Johannine community), Peter (apostolic churches), and those who deny that the Christ came in the flesh (Gnostics). See Raymond E. Brown, " 'Other Sheep Not of This Fold': The Johannine Perspective on Christian Diversity in the Late First Century," *Journal of Biblical Literature* 97 (1978): 5–22.

Scripture Index

Genesis

17	*56*

Exodus

13:11-13	*18*
20:2	*28*
22:21-24	*35*
22:29b	*18*
25-31; 35-40	*57*
25:40	*97*
34:14	*27*

Leviticus

17-26	*17*
23	*12*
25	*35*

Numbers

28-30	*12*

Joshua

9-10	*37*
24:14-28	*25-27*

Judges

3:7-11	*21*
3:15-30	*21*
4	*21*
5	*21*
6-8	*22*
8:22-23	*20*
9	*22*
9:7-15	*22*

1 Samuel

8:4-5	*23-24*
8:10-17	*23-24*
11	*40*
13:19-23	*39*
14:52	*40*

22:1-2	*40*
25	*41*
27	*41*
30:26	*41*

2 Samuel

5:1-3	*41*
5:6-10	*42*
5:11-12	*42*
6	*42*
7:14-15	*53*
8:15-18	*42*
8:17	*42*
15:1-6	*50*

1 Kings

4:21-23	*44*
4:26-28	*44*
5:13-15	*44*
6, 7	*44*
11:26-40	*45*
11:43	*45*
12:1-4	*45*
15, 20	*45*
18:21	*27*
22	*15*

2 Kings

5	*27*
9	*49*
23	*49*

1 Chronicles

7:1-15	*27*
14:7	*42*

Ezra

1:2-4	*58*
7:11-20	*59*
7:24	*59*

Psalms

2:7-9	*48*
24:9-10	*13*
29	*14*
45:6	*48*
47	*13, 14*
72:1-4	*50*
72:6	*48*
72:12-13	*50*
74:12-17	*11*
89:3-4	*47*
89:26-28	*47*
89:31-34	*47, 53*
89:35-36	*47*
93	*13, 14*
95-99	*13*
97:1-6	*16*
97:10	*16*
98:7-9	*17*
110:1, 4	*48*
132	*42*
132:7-8	*13*
132:13-15	*52*
146	*5*

Isaiah

1:10-17	*51*
1:21-26	*52*
2:1-5	*53*
5:8-10	*52*
6	*15*
6:10-13	*52*
6:13	*52*
7:10-13	*52*
9:1-6	*53*
10:1-4	*52*
10:32-34	*52*
11:1	*52*
11:1-4	*53*
11:9	*5*
14:28-32	*52*
32:1-5	*53*
32:15-20	*53*
42:1-4	*61*
45:1-7	*61*
49:6	*61*
52:7	*61*
55:1-5	*61*
58:3-4	*62*
61:1-3	*5*
65:17-25	*62*
66:1-2	*62*

Jeremiah

7:11	*83*

Ezekiel

45:1-12	*57*

Matthew

5:21-26	*81*
5:38-42	*81*
5:43-45	*81*
11:4-5	*4*
18:21-22	*82*
23:8-12	*77*
23:23	*78*
23:27-28	*78*

Mark

1:15	*72*
1:16-20	*73*
2:1-12	*74*
3:1-6	*74*
3:7, 13	*73*
3:31-35	*77*
4:11	*74*
4:35	*73*
6:7-13	*74*
8:31	*96*
9:1	*5*
10:17-22	*77*
10:23-25	*77*
10:28-31	*78*
10:45	*96*
11:17	*83*
13:1-2	*79*
14:1-2	*76*
14:3	*76*
14:28	*86*
15:7	*79*
16:7	*86*

Luke

4:18-19	*71*
6:20-26	*77*
10:1-12	*74*
13:22	*74*
14:25-27	*78*
16:19-31	*94*
17:11	*74*
18:31	*74*
19:11, 28	*74*
19:41, 45	*75*
24:25-26	*96*

John

1:1-14	*98*
3:3	*99*
3:16	*98*
18:36	*99*

Acts

1:9-11	*86*
2:44-45	*86*
2:46	*86*
3:1	*86*
3:17-21	*86*
4:34-35	*86*
6:8-7:1	*86*
7:2-53	*86*
7:54-60	*86*
21:17-26	*86*

Romans

5:12	*91*
5:6-9	*91*
6:3-5	*92*

1 Corinthians

1:17-31	*90*
2:2	*90*
6:9-10	*94*
7:21	*93*
15:50	*95*

Galatians

2:20	*90*
5:19-21	*95*

Colossians

3:11	*92*
4:1	*93*

Hebrews

9:11-14	*97*
12:18-21	*98*
12:28	*97*

1 John

4:1-3	*98*